Finger Foods

Finger Foods

appetizer, hors d'oeuvres, small plates and more

A Fireside Book
Published by Simon & Schuster
New York   London   Toronto   Sidney

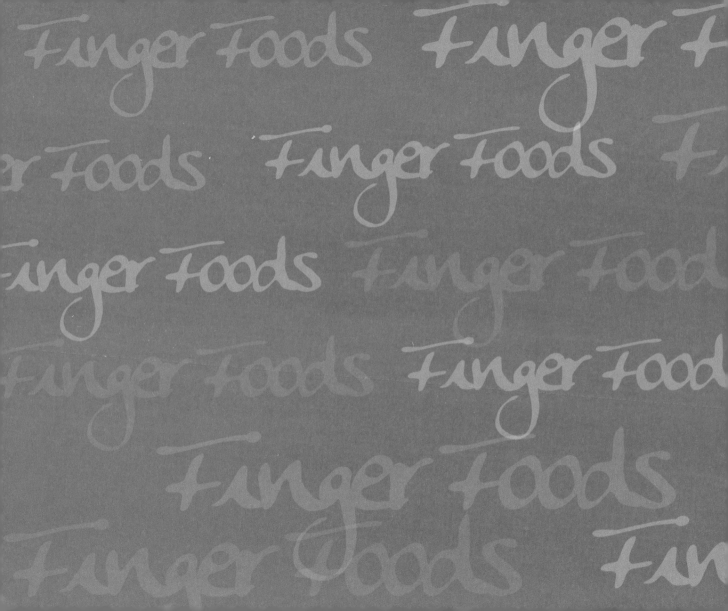

Summary

Stuzzichini

This Italian word describes a huge range of foods, savory and sweet, baked or fried, with just one thing in common: they can all be eaten with the hands. Nibbles with drinks, tapas, sushi, canapés and petits fours are just some examples of stuzzichini. Read on for advice on how to prepare and serve the best of them.

Finger Food

This term covers all kinds of little bites, nibbles and treats which can be eaten without the use of cutlery. This style of eating has recently experienced a surge in popularity, and now finger food has developed from just a hors-d'oeuvre or snack to a whole course or even a full meal, gaining new respect and status.

Not long ago, stuzzichini were served as the first element of the meal, with the aim of exciting diners' appetite (stuzzicare means "to excite" in Italian, as well as "to pick"), or outside mealtimes as a simple snack to restore energy.

In some countries, such as Spain, finger food has a long and glorious history. Tapas, literally "covers", are little snacks whose original function was to cover the carafe or glass of wine, protecting it from flies and other insects.

The Spanish are used to eating tapas at all hours of the day, and in their culture these pleasant little intermezzi often replace a meal, particularly during the hot summer months.

In Italy as well some stuzzichini have historical origins, such as the Tuscan or Campanian bruschetta, originally lunch or dinner for farmers and herders; or the Sicilian rice-balls called arancini; or focaccia, of which Liguria is the undisputed motherland.

a word of advice

Cured meats do not take well to long storage in the refrigerator, and risk losing their fragrance and flavor. They should be cut just before serving, or else one risks finding a breadstick, tartlet or bruschetta covered with a dry and tasteless slice of prosciutto, salami or coppa.

Today in Italy, with the growing tendency for happy hours and extended aperitivi often turning into dinner, these little dishes, initially the food of the poor and strictly regional, have now become refined delicacies, often using exotic spices or other sophisticated seasonings.

Canapés

The kind of bread used in canapés is of fundamental importance. It must have a soft but compact crumb, and be able to support toppings without losing its shape. For this reason, with some rare exceptions, it is best to use a rectangular sandwich loaf, with or without crusts.

Canapés can be topped with a wide range of ingredients, from the classic smoked salmon to prosciutto, from seafood to vegetables, usually all matched with a flavorful sauce or spread.

The sauce plays a key role, as the bread and many of the ingredients used can often be quite dry. This is why no self-respecting canapé will be without an accompanying sauce.

The only rules to follow in choosing ingredients are the classics: quality raw materials and good taste in pairing flavors.

An important note of advice on preparation, which should always take place as close as possible to serving: Avoid making canapés a day in advance, as they will become soggy, soft and decidedly unappetizing.

Additionally their appearance will certainly suffer over time. Instead, if necessary, prepare the sauces and other ingredients in advance (storing them carefully), then assemble the canapés at the last possible minute.

There is no doubt that dishes "made to order" have a great advantage in freshness and taste, whether pasta, risotto, meat or even simple appetizers.

another idea
If finger food and canapés are prepared in advance, cover them with aluminum foil. Plastic wrap is not recommended, as it can stick and cause condensation, which can spoil the food.

Finger Foods

7

Bruschette

How to resist the aroma of lightly toasted bread, seasoned with simple and tasty ingredients and enhanced by appetizing and flavorful sauces?

Brightly colored, crunchy and fragrant: This is what makes crostini and bruschette irresistible and essential to every good aperitivo or cocktail party.

Today crostini can be served warm or chilled. If warm, they are basically just small bruschette. If cold, they are in effect small panini made with toasted bread. In general there are a few essential rules to follow in preparing crostini. Of course, choose the best quality toppings, but it is also important to pay attention to matching the bread to the ingredients.

More delicate breads are suited to creams and purees of fish, ham or cheese, while more rustic breads pair well with sauces based on game meats, aged cheeses or other strongly flavored ingredients.

Then all that remains is to carefully follow the recipe and the rest is easy.

Sweet Stuzzichini

The range of small little sweets and petits fours has grown over the centuries to include an infinite number of variations, inspired by the imagination and creativity of pastry chefs around the world.

The success of these kinds of preparations comes from one key element, namely variety. In contrast to the majority of cakes and puddings, generally more than one kind of petit four is served, with different contrasting and complimentary preparations.

The classic spread of petits fours includes treats based on cream, chocolate and fruit, and can be a true feast for the eyes as well as the palate, with brightly colored glazes, soft creams, different kinds of chocolate, jellies and fruits of every kind, from the most common to the most exotic.

These are the basic foundations for various kinds of confectionery. It cannot be

a secret

It is always advisable to toast bread, apart from some multigrain varieties. Toasting makes bread tastier, and removes excess moisture. It also prepares the surface of the bread for any sauces or toppings, which would be overly absorbed by fresh bread.

denied that these sweets cannot feature heavily in a low-calorie diet. However it must be remembered that only excess is truly harmful, and that a few small infractions, while perhaps not satisfying the highest health standards, have on the other hand the indisputable benefit of gratifying us, restoring a good mood and a positive frame of mind which is more important than an impeccable ideal weight. We therefore call for a ban on overly rigorous and restrictive diets without sense or balance. A small daily dose of sweetness, within reason, perhaps during a break (whether in the office, at home or at school) will not ruin your diet, but will instead bring pleasure and relaxation.

Cooking

The timing and means of cooking are always of great importance to successfully preparing cookies, petits fours and other small after-hours treats.

Oven temperatures depend on the recipe and kind of preparation, and there are no immutable rules.

There are however certain guidelines to follow, with a few exceptions.

For example, puff pastry is usually baked in a very hot oven, well above 400°F (200°C or Gas Mark 6) as are many other kinds of pastry and brioche.

Another confectionery classic, babà, is usually baked around 400°F (200°C or Gas Mark 6), as are beignets, which are filled after baking.

Tea cakes and vol-au-vents are often baked around 300°F (150°C or Gas Mark 2). Finally the most fragrant biscuits and delicate meringues are baked at around 250°F (130°C or Gas Mark 1/2) and 210°F (100°C or Gas Mark 1/4) respectively. For all these preparations, apart from some exceptions, the sweets should be placed near the middle of the oven, where the heat is most evenly distributed. Generally flour should be sifted.

the basic rules

As a general rule, when preparing different doughs it is necessary to take care over the kind of flour used. In the majority of cases it should be white and rich in gluten.
This will make dough smooth, lump-free and easily rolled out and shaped.

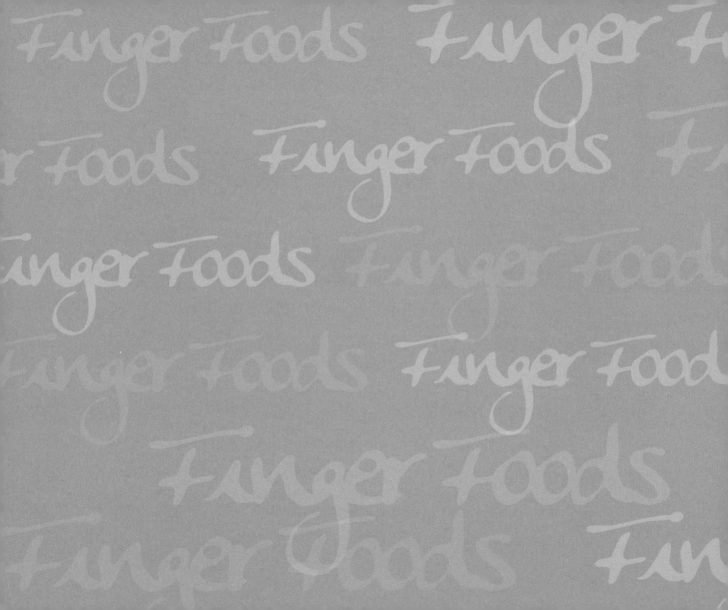

Contents

finger food

chestnut, ricotta and speck tartlets

Ingredients for 4 servings
Dough:

1 cup plus 3 tbsps (5½ oz or
150 g) all-purpose flour

5 tbsps (2½ ounces or 70 g) butter, diced

1 egg yolk, salt

Filling:

5½ oz (150 g) ricotta cheese

salt and pepper

1 thyme sprig, minced

1 tbsp light extra-virgin olive oil

4 tbsps (2 oz or 60 g) finely chopped
cooked chestnuts

2 oz (50 g) speck, thinly sliced and diced

Preheat the oven to 325°F (170°C or Gas Mark 3). Mound
the flour on a wooden board. Make a well in the center
and add the butter, egg yolk, salt and a little ice water.
Quickly mix the ingredients into a dough, gradually
adding a little bit of water if necessary.
As soon as the dough comes together wrap it in plastic
wrap and refrigerate for 30 minutes.
Meanwhile, beat the ricotta with salt, pepper, thyme
and olive oil. Add the chestnuts (reserve some
for garnish) and speck. Set aside in a cool place.
Roll out the dough and use it to line miniature tart tins.
Place a few dried beans in each tin to avoid air bubbles
while baking. Bake for 18 minutes or until golden-brown.
Remove from the oven and let cool.
Fill the tartlet shells with the ricotta mixture and garnish
with the reserved chopped chestnuts.

Chestnuts have been feeding people since
time immemorial. In the 5th century BC,
Xenophon described the chestnut as the
"tree of bread," and both Martial and
Virgil wrote about the consumption
and cultivation of the nuts.

Preparation time **25 minutes**
Cooking time **18 minutes**
Level **easy**

buffalo mozzarella and black olive panzerotti

Ingredients for 4 servings
Miniums Panzerotti:

2 tsps active dry yeast

salt and pepper

7 tbsps warm water

1 tsp lard

1½ cups (7 oz or 200 g)
all-purpose flour

1 buffalo mozzarella (9 oz or 250 g)

2 ripe tomatoes, chopped

thyme and basil, minced

fennel seeds

3 tbsps extra-virgin olive oil

2 tbsps pitted black olives, chopped

sunflower oil

For a lighter version, replace
the lard with 2 tbsps olive oil.

Mix the yeast and salt in the warm water, add the lard
and mix with the flour to make a dough. Let rest
for 1 hour, making an X-shaped incision on the surface
to allow rising.
Meanwhile cut the mozzarella into cubes and place
in a colander to drain. Toss the chopped tomatoes
with thyme, basil, fennel seeds, olive oil, salt and pepper.
Roll out the dough and cut out circles with a cookie cutter.
Fill with mozzarella and olives and fold over to make
half-moons. Press around the edges to seal.
Heat the sunflower oil until very hot and fry the panzerotti.
Drain on paper towels and serve with the tomatoes.

Preparation time **25 minutes**
Cooking time **5 minutes**
Level **easy**

spring rolls with crab, asparagus and carrot

Ingredients for 4 servings
Spring Rolls:

2 large crabs or 7 oz (200 g) crab meat

1/2 cup (120 ml) white wine (if using whole crabs), salt

juice and rind of **1** organic lemon (if using whole crabs)

8 small asparagus spears, peeled

1 tbsp extra-virgin olive oil

1 spring onion, minced, parsley, minced

12 square spring-roll wrappers

3 carrots, peeled and julienned

sunflower oil

If using whole crabs, bring 8 cups (2 litres) of water and the wine to a boil. Add salt and the crabs and bring to a simmer. Add the lemon juice and rind and cook for 10 minutes. Drain the crabs, crack their shells and remove the meat. Blanch the asparagus for 2 minutes in boiling water. Drain and cut into julienne strips.
Heat the olive oil in a frying pan and sauté the spring onion with a little water. Add the crab meat and parsley. Lay out the spring-roll wrappers. Place a 1-inch (3 cm) strip of asparagus and carrots along one side. Top with some crab mixture. Fold in the sides of the wrapper. Paint the edges of the wrapper with water using a small brush, then roll up tightly, pressing well to seal.
Let the spring rolls sit for 2 minutes. Meanwhile heat the sunflower oil until very hot. Fry the spring rolls until golden. Drain, salt and serve immediately.

"Crab" is the generic name given to various species of decapod crustaceans, which can live in rivers, the sea or on land. They are generally quite costly, and like lobsters the percentage of inedible material is high.

Preparation time **25 minutes**
Cooking time 1**5 minutes**
Level **easy**

pear pearls with parmesan and lime

Ingredients for 4 servings

Pear Pearls:

5 tbsps grated Parmesan cheese

grated zest of **1** organic lime

2 Williams pears

4 dried oregano stems

Mix together the Parmesan and lime zest. Peel the pears and cut them into balls using a melon baller. Dip the pear balls in the Parmesan mixture.

Remove any leaves from the oregano stems, and cut the stems with scissors into 1-inch (3 cm) lengths.

Stick a piece of stem into each pear ball, and arrange them on small individual plates to serve as an appetizer. Alternatively they can be passed as a cocktail snack.

For a more delicate taste, use aged ricotta salata, a softer and less pungent cheese, instead of Parmesan. The oregano stems can be replaced by toothpicks or rosemary sprigs with the leaves removed and the stem cut into short lengths.

Preparation time **10 minutes**

Level **easy**

phyllo cups with lentil cream

Ingredients for 4 servings

Phyllo Cups:

1 cup (7 oz or 200 g) lentils

salt

2 tbsps extra-virgin olive oil

1 shallot, minced

1 thyme sprig

1 roll phyllo dough

Soak the lentils in water for 8 hours. Preheat the oven to 400°F (200°C or Gas Mark 6).
Drain the lentils and boil them in salted water until soft. Meanwhile heat the olive oil in a small frying pan and sauté the shallot.
When the lentils are cooked, drain them and add to the shallot. Sauté for a few minutes, then add the thyme leaves. Puree the lentils in a food processor and keep warm.
Roll out the phyllo dough, two layers at a time, and cut it into circles with a cookie cutter. Use the circles to line small cylindrical molds or paper baking cups.
Place a few dried beans in each one to stop the dough from puffing up, then bake until browned and crispy. Remove from the oven and let cool.
Unmold and serve filled with the lentil puree.

Lentils are rich in calcium, phosphorous and iron and have many uses in the kitchen. The most famous Italian lentils are from Umbria, grown on the high Castelluccio plateau in Norcia. Like all dried legumes, lentils benefit from being soaked in water for a few hours before cooking.

Preparation time **20 minutes**
Cooking time **30 minutes**
Level **easy**

mushrooms stuffed
with tomato and ricotta

Ingredients for 4 servings
Mushrooms:

salt and pepper

1/2 cup (120 ml) white wine, **1** bay leaf

12 very fresh medium-sized mushrooms

2 tbsps extra-virgin olive oil

1 garlic clove

1 slice of sandwich bread

1 tsp tomato concentrate

1 oz (30 g) ricotta salata, shaved

oregano (optional)

For a tomato-free filling, prepare the mushroom stalks as above, but without the tomato concentrate. Add 3½ oz (100 g) fresh goat's milk ricotta and some fresh minced herbs (parsley, oregano, basil, thyme) to the mushroom puree and season with salt and pepper. Garnish with a strip of roasted red pepper in oil.

Bring 4 cups (1 l) of salted water to a boil with the wine and bay leaf.
Clean the mushrooms and remove and reserve the stalks. Blanch the mushroom caps for 4-5 minutes in the seasoned water. Drain and let dry on a clean kitchen towel. Meanwhile heat the olive oil and garlic clove in a frying pan. Add the mushrooms stalks and sauté for 5-6 minutes. Season with salt to taste and transfer to a food processor with the bread and tomato concentrate.
Puree until smooth, then adjust salt and pepper.
Fill each mushroom cap with 1 tablespoon of filling. Garnish with ricotta salata shavings, and sprinkle with oregano and pepper if desired.

Preparation time **15 minutes**
Cooking time **10 minutes**
Level **easy**

savory strudel with escarole, goat's cheese and anchovies

Ingredients for 4 servings

Dough:

1 cup plus 3 tbsps (5½ oz or 150 g) all-purpose flour

1/2 cup (2 oz or 60 g) emmer flour

2 tbsps extra-virgin olive oil, salt

Filling:

1 head escarole

2 tbsps extra-virgin olive oil

2 garlic cloves, peeled and smashed

1/2 red chili pepper, salt and pepper

2 tbsps breadcrumbs

6½ oz (180 g) fresh goat's cheese

6 anchovy fillets in oil, drained and finely chopped

Sift together the two flours and mound them on a wooden pastry board. Make a well in the center and pour in the olive oil and a little warm water with some salt dissolved in it. Mix together to make an elastic dough.
Form into a ball and refrigerate for 30 minutes.
Preheat the oven to 350°F (180°C or Gas Mark 4).
Remove the leaves from the head of escarole and wash them in cold water. Drain, leaving the leaves wet. Heat the oil in a frying pan and sauté the garlic cloves and chili pepper. Add the escarole, season with a little salt and pepper, and cook until the escarole is soft and any liquid has evaporated. Roll the dough out on a floured work surface. Sprinkle with breadcrumbs. Cover with the sautéed escarole. Sprinkled over pieces of goat's cheese and the chopped anchovies.
Roll up the strudel and cut a series on incisions along the top. Brush with olive oil and bake for 20 minutes.
Serve hot.

For slightly different flavor, replace the goat's cheese with another fresh cheese with a lighter flavor.

Preparation time **20 minutes**
Cooking time **40 minutes**
Level **easy**

pea cream with tempeh crisps

Ingredients for 4 servings

Pea Cream:

5½ oz (150 g) phyllo dough

extra-virgin olive oil

1/2 onion, minced

1½ cups (7 oz or 200 g) peas

salt and pepper

1/2 cup (120 ml) heavy cream

sunflower oil

2 oz (50 g) tempeh, thinly sliced

Preheat the oven to 350°F (180°C or Gas Mark 4).
Lay three layers of phyllo dough on top of each other, brushing each layer with olive oil.
Cut into 1½-inch (4 cm) squares and use to line small tartlet molds. Bake for 10-15 minutes. Heat some olive oil in a frying pan and sauté the onion. Add the peas, salt and pepper and sauté for a few minutes. Add 1/2 cup (120 ml) water and cook, covered, for 20 minutes.
Puree the peas in a food processor and let cool.
Whip the cream, then fold it into the cooled pea puree. Heat the sunflower oil and fry the slices of tempeh until crisp. Drain and dry on paper towels. Sprinkle with salt. Fill the phyllo shells with the pea cream and garnish with fried tempeh crisps.
Serve immediately.

Tempeh is made from steamed soy beans which are then left to ferment after a mycelium has been added. A very digestible food, it can be cooked on the grill, fried, stewed with vegetables, baked, skewered or made into vegetarian meatballs.

Preparation time **20 minutes**
Cooking time **30 minutes**
Level **easy**

mini spiced triangles

Ingredients for 4 servings
Mini Spiced:

3 tbsps extra-virgin olive oil

1 onion, minced, **2** bay leaves

20 sheets of briq dough

1 egg, beaten, sunflower oil

1 lb (500 g) ground beef

2 garlic cloves, minced

1 bunch coriander, destemmed and
finely chopped

1 tsp ground ginger

1 tsp turmeric

salt and pepper

Heat the olive oil in a heavy-bottomed saucepan and sauté the onion and bay leaves. Add the ground beef, garlic, ginger, turmeric, salt and pepper and continue cooking for 30 minutes, adding the coriander about halfway through. Remove the bay leaves and let cool.
Cut the briq dough sheets in half to obtain narrow rectangles. Place a small spoonful of beef at the end of each rectangle and fold it over in triangles until reaching the end of the dough strip.
Brush the end with a little beaten egg and press to seal. Heat the sunflower oil until hot, then fry the triangles. Drain on paper towels and serve immediately

Sometimes known as Chinese parsley, coriander is an ancient herb with a long history. According to Pliny, placing a few coriander seeds under one's pillow will cure fever and headache.

Preparation time **20 minutes**
Cooking time **40 minutes**
Level **easy**

mini tofu kebabs with cherry tomatoes and baby zucchini

Ingredients for 4 servings
Kebabs:

8 small baby zucchini
1 block tofu, cut into cubes
16 cherry tomatoes
2 tbsps extra-virgin olive oil
salt

Sauce:

2 tbsps tomato sauce
1 tbsp rice malt
1 tbsp sweet paprika
1 tbsp extra-virgin olive oil
Tabasco sauce

To make tofu more digestible,
before use boil it in water
for 7 minutes, then drain
and cut according to the recipe.

Preheat the oven to 400°F (200°C or Gas Mark 6).
Trim the zucchini and cut them in half along the diagonal.
Line a baking tray with greaseproof paper.
Thread a piece of tofu, a piece of zucchini and a cherry
tomato onto a toothpick. Repeat to make 16 mini kebabs.
Arrange them standing up on the baking tray.
Drizzle with oil, sprinkle over a little salt and bake
for 10 minutes.
Meanwhile mix together all the sauce ingredients,
adding Tabasco to taste. Serve the kebabs with the sauce.

Preparation time **10 minutes**
Cooking time **10 minutes**
Level **easy**

coconut chicken nuggets

Ingredients for 4 servings
Coconut Chicken Nuggets:

1 chicken breast, cut into small chunks

juice of **1** lemon

4-5 mint leaves, roughly chopped

salt and pepper

4 tbsps all-purpose flour

cold sparkling water

2/3 cup (3½ oz or 100 g) shredded coconut

sunflower oil

Place the chicken in a bowl with the lemon juice, mint, salt and pepper. Stir well and let sit for 20 minutes. Drain the chicken and pat dry with paper towels. Discard the mint. Mix together the all-purpose flour and enough cold sparkling water to make a thin batter. Add the chicken pieces and toss to coat.
Press the batter on by hand if necessary, then dip the pieces in the shredded coconut.
Heat the sunflower oil and fry the chicken nuggets until golden-brown. Drain on paper towels, sprinkle with salt and serve immediately.

For an even more exotic flavor, use the juice of only 1/2 lemon, and add 1 tsp ginger juice to the marinade. Ginger juice can be made by squeezing grated ginger in a piece of muslin.

Preparation time **20 minutes**
Cooking time **10 minutes**
Level **easy**

quinoa and porcini croquettes

Ingredients for 4 servings

Croquettes:

4 cups (1 l) light vegetable broth

3 tbsps extra-virgin olive oil

1 large shallot, minced

1½ cups (9 oz or 250 g) quinoa

2 fresh porcini mushrooms

1 garlic clove, smashed

parsley, minced, salt and pepper

1 egg, beaten

3/4 cup (3½ oz or 100 g) breadcrumbs

sunflower oil

The fresh porcini can be replaced by 4 oz (120 g) dried porcini. Before use, soak for about 30 minutes in water, then drain.

Bring the vegetable broth to a boil. Heat 1 tablespoon of olive oil in a heavy-bottomed saucepan and sauté the shallot. Add the quinoa and toast briefly, then add the boiling vegetable broth.

Meanwhile clean the porcini by removing the earthy part of the stalk and brushing the cap with a damp paper towel, then thinly slice them. Heat the remaining olive oil with the garlic and sauté the porcini over high heat, sprinkling them with minced parsley. Transfer the sautéed mushrooms to a cutting board and chop them roughly. Add the mushrooms to the quinoa while it is still cooking. As soon as the quinoa is cooked, transfer the mixture to a bowl and let cool. Season to taste with salt and pepper. Form the quinoa-mushroom mixture into small balls by hand, dampening the hands with cold water to prevent sticking. Refrigerate the quinoa balls for 15 minutes. Dip the balls in beaten egg and then in breadcrumbs. Heat the sunflower oil until very hot and fry the croquettes, turning carefully until evenly browned. Drain on paper towels and lightly salt. Serve immediately.

Preparation time **20 minutes**
Cooking time **10 minutes**
Level **easy**

pear skewers with honey and gorgonzola

Ingredients for 4 servings

Skewers:

2 Williams pears

1½ tbsps (3/4 oz or 20 g) butter

2 tsps acacia honey

freshly ground pepper

5½ oz (150 g) mild, semi-aged

Gorgonzola cheese

In the Lombardian town of Gorgonzola the milk from tired (stracche or fatigued) cows was used to make stracchino cheese, also known as crescenza. According to legend some forms of stracchino were forgotten in the cellar of a tavern and were "ruined" by green mould. This new cheese was immediately appreciated by the local drinkers and named after its town of origin.

Peel the pears and cut them into 4 wedges. Remove the central core and cut the wedges into small cubes, about 1/2-inch (1 cm) each side.

Melt the butter in a large non-stick frying pan.

Gently brown the pear cubes, drizzling over the honey and turning often until caramelized. Sprinkle with a little freshly ground pepper and then transfer to a tray lined with parchment paper.

Cut the Gorgonzola into cubes the same size as the pears and create miniature skewers by threading alternating pear and cheese cubes onto toothpicks.

Serve as a starter, or paired with a good glass of wine as a pre-dinner snack.

Preparation time **15 minutes**
Cooking time **10 minutes**
Level **easy**

citrus chicken tempura

Ingredients for 4 servings
Tempura:

1 large chicken breast

juice of **1** lemon, salt and pepper

grated zest of **1** organic lime

3/4 cup (3½ oz or 100 g)
all-purpose flour

2 tbsps rice flour

1/2 tsp baking soda

very cold sparkling water

1 tbsp poppy seeds, sunflower oil

lemon leaves for garnish (optional)

Cut the chicken into small pieces, about 1-inch (2 cm) each, then place in a bowl with the lemon juice, pepper and grated lime zest. Stir, then refrigerate for 4 hours.
Sift the two flours in a bowl and add the baking soda. Using a fork or a whisk, stir in enough cold sparkling water to form a smooth and fluid batter.
Stir in the poppy seeds. Heat abundant sunflower oil in a wok. Drain the chicken and pat dry on paper towels. Toss the chicken pieces in the batter, then drain, tapping on the side of the bowl to remove excess batter,
and fry in the hot oil until golden.
Drain on paper towels and lightly salt.
Serve hot, garnished with lemon leaves, if desired.

Did you know that the fruit of the poppy plant, an egg-shaped capsule, contains more than 20,000 tiny seeds, from which poppyseed oil is extracted? If a cut is made in the capsule before it matures, a milky fluid seeps out, which condenses when exposed to air. This is the raw material for opium.

Preparation time **20 minutes**
Cooking time **20 minutes**
Level **easy**

pineapple and marinated salmon kebabs

Ingredients for 4 servings
Salmon Kebabs:

14 oz (400 g) salmon fillet
1/2 ripe pineapple
3 tbsps apple vinegar
1 tsp soy sauce
1 tsp sugar
salt and white pepper
1 tbsp extra-virgin olive oil
1 tsp sesame seeds
lemon thyme (optional)

Remove the skin and any bones from the salmon. Cut the fillet into cubes about 1/2-inch (1½ cm) on each side. Remove the peel from the pineapple and cut it into 4 slices 1/2-inch (1½ cm) thick. Cut these into strips and then into cubes the same size as the salmon cubes. Whisk together the apple vinegar, soy sauce, sugar, salt and pepper. Whisk in the extra-virgin olive oil in a thin stream to emulsify. Toss the salmon with the sauce and let sit for 10 minutes. Drain the salmon. Thread the salmon and pineapple cubes onto short wooden skewers or toothpicks. Grill them on a pre-heated non-stick grill pan for 30 seconds on each side, sprinkling them with sesame seeds as they cook.
Serve warm, garnished with lemon thyme if desired.

The unusual combination of pineapple and salmon proves to be very successful, as the richness of the salmon is undercut by the acidic, juicy pineapple.

Preparation time **15 minutes**
Cooking time **1 minute**
Level **easy**

vegetable tempura with kombu

Ingredients for 4 servings

Tempura:

very cold sparkling water

1 cup plus 3 tbsps (5½ oz or 150 g) all-purpose flour

sunflower oil

1 leek, julienned

2 carrots, julienned

2 zucchini, julienned

1 fennel bulb, julienned

4 broccoli florets, thinly sliced

2 sheets of kombu seaweed, julienned

Whisk enough cold sparkling water into the flour to obtain a fluid but dense batter.
Heat the sunflower oil. Toss the vegetables and kombu in the batter and then fry them in the hot oil.
Drain on paper towels and serve hot.

Kombu is a brown seaweed, rich in minerals. It is cooked together with vegetables to make them softer and more digestible. Kombu contains glutamic acid, the basis of the flavor enhancer monosodium glutamate.

Preparation time **10 minutes**
Cooking time 1**5 minutes**
Level **easy**

mixed sushi

Ingredients for 4 servings
Sushi:

2 cups (14 oz or 400 g) rice

1 tbsp sugar, **1** tsp salt

3 tbsps white vinegar, **1** tbsp sake

3 sheets nori seaweed

4 oz (120 g) fresh swordfish fillet,
cut lengthwise into thin strips

4 oz (120 g) fresh tuna fillet,
cut lengthwise into thin strips

1 cucumber, julienned

4 oz (120 g) fresh salmon fillet,
cut lengthwise into thin strips

4 tbsps fresh minced ginger

2 tsps horseradish, soy sauce

pickled cucumbers (optional)

Boil the rice until cooked, then drain. Mix together the sugar, salt, vinegar and sake, and toss with the warm rice. Lay a sheet of nori on a damp cloth. Spread a third of the rice over the seaweed, leaving a 1-inch (2 cm) border around the two longer edges.
Make a line of swordfish strips down the middle of the rice. Roll the seaweed up tightly to form a compact roll. Repeat with the other sheets, filling one with the tuna strips and half the cucumber, and the other with the salmon strips and the remaining cucumber.
Let the rolls rest for at least 1 hour, then cut them into 2½–inch (3-4 cm) lengths.
Mix together the ginger and horseradish and roll into 8 small balls. Dip half the balls in soy sauce. Serve the sushi with the ginger balls and soy sauce, garnished if desired with pickled cucumbers.

Preparation time **20 minutes**
Cooking time **15 minutes**
Level **medium**

nigiri sushi

Ingredients for 4 servings

Sushi:

2 cups (14 oz or 400 g) sushi rice

1 piece kombu seaweed, salt, 1 tsp sugar

2 tbsps Japanese rice vinegar, 1 egg

4 oz (125 g) fresh salmon fillet,
skin removed, thinly sliced

3½ oz (100 g) fresh tuna fillet from
the top part, thinly sliced

3 oz (80 g) fresh sea bass fillet,
thinly sliced

4 cooked shrimp, peeled and
opened like a book

1 octopus tentacle, cooked and
thinly sliced

wasabi, soy sauce, pickled ginger

The rich variety of ingredients used in
nigiri sushi (different kinds of seafood
and eggs) together with the rice makes it
almost a complete meal in itself.

Wash the rice under running water and let it drain.
Soak for 10 minutes in a saucepan with 1½ cups (350 ml)
water and the kombu seaweed. Bring to a boil and cook
on high heat for 2 minutes. Lower the heat and let cook,
covered, for 15 minutes, until cooked through.
Meanwhile whisk the salt and sugar into the rice vinegar
until dissolved. Remove the rice from the heat, cover
with a kitchen towel and let cool for another 10 minutes.
Sprinkle a hangiri or wooden tray with cold water and
transfer the rice to it. Stir with a flat wooden spatula.
Pour over the vinegar mixture and keep stirring for about
10 minutes, then cover with a damp kitchen towel so that
it does not dry out.
Beat the egg and cook in a small non-stick frying pan
to make a small omelet. Cut into slices.
With damp hands, form small balls of rice into rectangles
and cover each one with either a thin slice of raw fish,
a shrimp, a slice of octopus or a slice of omelet.
Serve with wasabi, soy sauce and pickled ginger.

Preparation time **20 minutes**
Cooking time **20 minutes**
Level **easy**

greek yogurt vol-au-vents with olives

Ingredients for 4 servings
Vol-au-Vents:
3 pickles
10 black olives, pitted
17 mint leaves
5½ oz (150 g) Greek yogurt
salt and pepper
1 tbsp extra-virgin olive oil
12 prepared vol-au-vents

Rinse the pickels and chop roughly. Mince half the olives and 5 mint leaves. Mix the chopped pickels, olives and mint into the yogurt together with salt, pepper and olive oil. Slice the remaining olives.
Fill the vol-au-vents with the yogurt mixture and top with 1 olive slice and 1 mint leaf.

Antoine Carême is credited with inventing the vol-au-vent, a small hollow case of puff pastry. Its name, which means "flying in the wind" in French, refers to its amazing lightness.

Preparation time **5 minutes**
Level **easy**

ham and fontina panzerotti

Ingredients for 4 servings
Panzerotti:

1 tsp active dry yeast

6 tbsps warm water

2 tbsps extra-virgin olive oil

salt and pepper

1½ cups plus 1½ tbsps
(7 oz or 200 g) all-purpose flour

5½ oz (150 g) ham, diced

3½ oz (100 g) fontina cheese, diced

sunflower oil

Dissolve the yeast in the warm water and stir in the olive oil, salt and pepper. Mound the flour on a wooden pastry board and make a well in the center.

Pour in the water and work with the palms of the hands to make a smooth and elastic dough.

Place the dough in a bowl, cover with a damp cloth and let rise. Flour a work surface and roll the dough out with a rolling pin. Mix together the ham and fontina.

Place little piles of the mixture, evenly spaced, on half of the dough. Fold over the over half, and cut out little circles around the filling using a round cookie cutter.

Heat the sunflower oil until very hot and fry the panzerotti. Drain on paper towels, lightly salt and serve hot.

The fontina can be replaced by a good melting mozzarella for pizza, or cheese slices. For a lighter snack, place the uncooked panzerotti on a baking sheet oiled with extra-virgin olive oil and then bake for about 18 minutes in a 400°F (200°C or Gas Mark 6) oven.

Preparation time **20 minutes**
Cooking time **10 minutes**
Level **easy**

crunchy quinoa bites

Ingredients for 4 servings

Crunchy:

3/4 cup (5½ oz or 150 g) quinoa

1¾ cups (400 ml) vegetable broth

2 large fresh porcini mushrooms (about 6½ oz or 180 g)

1 tbsp extra-virgin olive oil, **1** garlic clove

1 thyme sprig, minced

1 tsp minced parsley, salt and pepper

3 tbsps breadcrumbs

2 tbsps gomasio (sesame salt)

sunflower oil

Quinoa is an annual plant, cultivated for millennia in the Andes. It produces tiny seeds, collected in bunches, which are edible only after being boiled or toasted. They can be ground into a flour which can be used together with wheat flour to make bread.

Rinse the quinoa well to remove any impurities. Place in a saucepan and cook for 2 minutes, stirring with a wooden spoon, to lightly toast. Add the vegetable broth and cook over low heat for 25 minutes.

Let sit for another 10 minutes. Clean the mushrooms with a damp cloth and slice them. Heat the olive oil and garlic in a frying pan and sauté the mushrooms over medium heat for 10 minutes. Adjust salt and pepper and add the parsley and thyme.

Mix the mushrooms and quinoa together. Form the quinoa mixture into small balls and refrigerate them for at least 20 minutes.

Dip the quinoa balls in a mixture of breadcrumbs and gomasio, then fry in hot sunflower oil and serve immediately.

Preparation time **25 minutes**

Cooking time **45 minutes**

Level **easy**

sea bream parcels

Ingredients for 4 servings
Parcels:

2 yellow-fleshed potatoes

salt and pepper

4 sea bream fillets (4 oz or 120 g each),
bones removed

2 thyme sprigs, leaves only

1 garlic clove

1 tbsp extra-virgin olive oil

Sauce:

1 bunch basil, **1** tbsp peanuts

5 tbsps extra-virgin olive oil

Peel the potatoes, thinly slice them and then cut into sticks, or grate the whole peeled potatoes. Lightly salt the sea bream filets. Cover the side without skin with thyme leaves and potatoes. Place the fillets in a non-stick frying pan with the garlic and olive oil. Salt and pepper, then cook on high heat for 3 minutes. Turn over and cook for another 2 minutes. To make the sauce, puree the basil, peanuts and olive oil in a food processor. Serve the sea bream parcels cut into small pieces, with the basil sauce.

Apart from its many culinary uses, thyme has also been used as a medicinal herb. Its essential oil is an antiseptic, and a thyme infusion is believed to help coughs and bronchitis.

Preparation time **15 minutes**
Cooking time **5 minutes**
Level **easy**

fried shrimp with stir-fried vegetables

Ingredients for 4 servings

Shrimp:

1 tsp active dry yeast

4½ tbsps warm water, salt

3/4 cup (3½ oz or 100 g)
all-purpose flour

1 pinch of baking soda, sunflower oil

12 jumbo shrimp, shelled

Vegetables:

1 tbsp sesame oil, **3** zucchini, julienned

2 tbsps extra-virgin olive oil

1 spring onion, minced

3 carrots, peeled and julienned

1 tsp white sesame seeds

1 tsp black sesame seeds, salt

Dissolve the yeast in the warm water and add a little salt.
Mix together the flour and baking soda, then pour
over the yeast mixture. Mix until smooth then let rise
for 1 hour.
Meanwhile heat the sesame oil and olive oil for the
vegetables in a wok. Sauté the spring onion.
Add the carrots and then the zucchini. Add the sesame
seeds and salt and sauté for 6 minutes over high heat.
Keep warm. Heat the sunflower oil.
Dip the shrimp in the risen batter and then fry them
in the hot oil until golden. Drain on paper towels and salt.
Serve over the stir-fried vegetables.

A wok is a round-bottomed iron cooking
vessel, used particularly in Chinese cuisine.
It allows foods which have been cut into
small pieces to be cooked very quickly.

Preparation time **20 minutes**
Cooking time **15 minutes**
Level **easy**

crescenza fritters with mortadella

Ingredients for 4 servings

Crescenza Fritters:

6½ oz (180 g) fresh crescenza cheese

1¾ cups (8 oz or 220 g) self-rising flour

2-3 sage leaves, finely minced

sunflower oil

salt

5½ oz (150 g) mortadella, thinly sliced

rosemary leaves (optional)

Beat the crescenza in a bowl with a fork until creamy. Add a little warm water and incorporate. Add the flour and stir with a spoon, adding water until the mixture has a gluey, stringy consistency. Add the sage and cover the bowl with aluminum foil. Let rise for about 40 minutes. Once the batter has risen, heat the sunflower oil. Using 2 tablespoons dipped in cold water, form small portions of batter and fry them in the oil. Once golden and puffed up, drain on paper towels. Salt lightly and serve with mortadella, garnished with rosemary leaves if desired.

The self-rising flour can be replaced with the same amount of all-purpose flour mixed with 1 tsp of baking powder.

Preparation time **15 minutes**
Cooking time **5 minutes**
Level **easy**

vegetable flan

Ingredients for 4 servings
Flan:

1⅓ lb (600 g) mixed vegetables (cabbage, zucchini, mushrooms, peas, green beans), chopped
3 tbsps extra-virgin olive oil
1 onion, minced, **1** carrot, minced
3½ oz (100 g) ham, diced
3½ tbsps (2 oz or 50 g) butter, softened
3/4 cup (3½ oz or 100 g) all-purpose flour
4 cups (1 l) milk, **1** tsp sugar
salt, nutmeg, grated
2 eggs, beaten, breadcrumbs
2-3 bay leaves

Preheat the oven to 350°F (180°C or Gas Mark 4).
Blanch all the mixed vegetables until tender.
Heat 2 tablespoons olive oil in a heavy-bottomed saucepan and sauté the onion and carrot. Add the mixed vegetables and ham and sauté for a few minutes.
Mix together the butter and flour. Heat the milk and add the butter-flour mixture, and stir until dissolved. Add the hot milk mixture to the vegetables and ham together with the sugar, a pinch of salt and a little grated nutmeg. Let thicken over low heat, stirring carefully, for about 10 minutes. Remove from the heat and add the eggs. Oil a cake tin with the remaining olive oil. Sprinkle with breadcrumbs, and pour in the vegetable mixture. Level off the surface and lay the bay leaves on top. Bake for 40-45 minutes. Unmold and slice before serving. This makes a good accompaniment to a stew or fish dish.

Nutmeg became a famous spice at the start of the 16th century with the discovery of the Spice Islands, now the Moluccas. Its sweet, refined flavor and woodsy perfume has made it a spice with an almost magical reputation and great prestige.

Preparation time **20 minutes**
Cooking time **1 hour 10 minutes**
Level **easy**

Finger Food

crunchy cannoli with ricotta and olives

Ingredients for 4 servings

Cannoli:

10½ oz (300 g) fresh ricotta

1 tbsp heavy cream, salt and pepper

2 tbsps extra-virgin olive oil, oregano

4 sheets phyllo dough, sunflower oil

1/2 cup (2 oz or 60 g) pitted black olives, minced

Sauce:

2 tbsps extra-virgin olive oil

2 garlic cloves, smashed, tomatoes, salt

1⅓ cups (9 oz or 250 g) canned chopped

Garnish:

Ligurian pesto (optional)

Black olives are harvested when very ripe, and then processed in various ways to make them softer. Usually they are then dried in the sun or baked before being preserved in oil.

Make the sauce by heating the olive oil and sautéing the garlic cloves. Add the tomatoes and cook until thickened. Remove the garlic, adjust salt and puree in a food processor or blender. Strain the mixture and keep warm. Beat the ricotta with the heavy cream, olive oil, salt, pepper and oregano.
Cut the phyllo dough into 2-inch (5 cm) strips and roll them around stainless-steel cannoli molds. Brush the edges with water and press to seal. Let dry for 1 minute. Heat the sunflower oil and fry the cannoli until golden. Drain on paper towels. Unmold the cannoli and fill them halfway full with the ricotta cream, using a pastry bag. Put 1 teaspoon of minced olives in the middle, then fill up with ricotta cream.
Serve the cannoli over the tomato sauce, garnished with a drizzle of Ligurian pesto, if desired.

Preparation time **30 minutes**
Cooking time **25 minutes**
Level **easy**

pepper rolls on escarole with feta

Ingredients for 4 servings
Rolls:

1 red bell pepper, **1** green bell pepper
1 yellow bell pepper, **1** garlic clove
6 tbsps extra-virgin olive oil
1/2 dried red chili pepper
1/2 head escarole, shredded
1/2 head lettuce, shredded
salt and pepper
4 thick slices Altamura-style bread
5½ oz (150 g) feta cheese

Preheat the oven to 425°F (220°C or Gas Mark 7). Cut the peppers in half and remove the stalk, seeds and white pith. Brush with a little olive oil and roast in the oven for about 12 minutes. Remove from the oven and close in a plastic bag to steam. Peel when cool.
Heat 3 tablespoons olive oil in a saucepan with the garlic and chili. Add the escarole and lettuce and sauté over high heat, adding a little water if necessary.
Season with salt and pepper to taste.
Cut the bread into 1/2-inch (1 cm) wide strips, making a total of 18 strips. Brush with olive oil, sprinkle with salt and toast in the oven. Cut each roast pepper half into three strips, and roll each strip around a piece of bread.
Serve the pepper rolls at room temperature over the sautéed escarole mixture, topped with crumbled feta and some pepper.

Altamura bread originally comes from Puglia and is made from flour ground from hard wheat of the Appulo, Arcangelo, Duilio and Simeto varieties. In 2003 it received a DOP (protected denomination of origin) designation.

Preparation time **15 minutes**
Cooking time **25 minutes**
Level **easy**

Finger Food

pumpkin and pea parcels

Ingredients for 4 servings

Parcels:

2 tbsps extra-virgin olive oil

1/4 onion, diced

1/2 pumpkin, diced

3/4 cup (180 ml) vegetable broth

salt and pepper

2 cups (10½ oz or 300 g) peas

9 oz (250 g) puff pastry

1 egg, beaten

1 tsp poppy seeds

Preheat the oven to 400°F (200°C or Gas Mark 6).
Heat the oil in a heavy-bottomed saucepan and sauté the onion with a spoonful of water.
Add the pumpkin and vegetable broth. Season with salt and pepper to taste and add the peas.
Cook over medium heat for 10 minutes, then let cool.
Cut the puff pastry into squares and fill them with the pumpkin mixture. Fold in the corners to make little parcels. Brush with beaten egg and sprinkle with poppy seeds.
Bake for 15 minutes. Serve hot or warm.

A good pumpkin should be fresh, well-ripened and firm. Test it by giving it a little knock; the sound should be dull, as though it was hollow.

Preparation time **30 minutes**
Cooking time **30 minutes**
Level **easy**

meatball kebabs with peonies

Ingredients for 4 servings
Meatball Kebabs:

1 small dry bread roll

1/2 cup (120 ml) milk

10½ oz (300 g) ground beef

3½ oz (100 g) ham, finely minced

2 tbsps grated Parmesan cheese, **1** egg

salt and pepper, **7** peony flowers

2/3 cup (3 oz or 80 g) all-purpose flour

sunflower oil, baby spinach leaves

Soak the bread roll in the milk until soft, then drain, squeeze out excess liquid and crumble into small pieces. Mix together the ground beef, ham, Parmesan and soaked bread. Mix in the egg, salt and pepper and stir until combined. Thinly slice half the peony petals and mix into the beef mixture.

Form the beef mixture into small walnut-sized balls. Dip into the flour. Heat the sunflower oil in a frying pan and fry the meatballs. Drain and dry on paper towels. Thread the meatballs onto kebab sticks, alternating them with peony petals and baby spinach leaves. Serve warm or chilled.

Peonies have edible flowers, with different flavors depending on the color. Yellow and lactiflora peonies have a peppery taste, while the other varieties have a delicate, honeyed flavor. The petals are delicious in avocado salads, battered and fried, used as an aromatic bed for fish or to season fillings.

Preparation time **15 minutes**
Cooking time **10 minutes**
Level **easy**

rosemary and cheese crackers

Ingredients for 4 servings
Crackers:

1/2 cup (3½ oz or 100 g)
cold butter, diced

2 oz (50 g) Emmenthal cheese

5 tbsps grated Parmesan cheese

1 cup (4 oz or 120 g) all-purpose flour

salt and pepper

2 tbsps rosemary flowers

rosemary sprigs

Quickly mix together the butter, Emmenthal, Parmesan and flour to form a dough.
Season with salt and pepper and mix in the rosemary flowers. Roll the dough in a sheet of parchment paper, forming a 1½-inch (4-centimeter) diameter roll. Refrigerate for at least 30 minutes.
Preheat the oven to 350°F (180°C or Gas Mark 4). Remove the paper and cut the roll into slices 1/3-inch (1 cm) thick. Lay them on a baking tray and bake for around 15 minutes.
Let cool and serve garnished with rosemary sprigs.

These crackers are delicious as a snack with drinks, or as an alternative to sweet cookies with tea. They will keep for a week in an air-tight container. They can also be topped with a mixture of ricotta, minced dill and minced gherkins.

Preparation time **10 minutes**
Cooking time **15 minutes**
Level **easy**

cheese twists

Ingredients for 4 servings

Twists:

1 lb (500 g) fresh cheese, such as feta

1 pinch dried mint

parsley, minced

1 lb (500 g) puff pastry

3½ tbsps (2 oz or 50 g) butter, melted

Garnish:

fresh mint or parsley leaves (optional)

Preheat the oven to 325°F (170°C or Gas Mark 3).
Break up the cheese with a fork.
Add the mint and parsley. Cut the puff pastry into rectangles or strips about 4-inches (10 cm) wide. Sprinkle 1 tablespoon of cheese over each one and twist up the pastry. Brush with melted butter and bake for about 20 minutes. Arrange the twists on plate and serve hot, garnished with fresh mint leaves or parsley, as desired.

Mint varieties used in the kitchen include spearmint and peppermint. When dried, mint loses much of its aromatic properties, and so is generally best used fresh.

Preparation time **15 minutes**
Cooking time **20 minutes**
Level **easy**

saffron arancini

Ingredients for 6 servings
Saffron:

4 tbsps extra-virgin olive oil

1/2 onion, minced

3/4 cup (5½ oz or 150 g) Carnaroli rice

1 pinch saffron

2 cups (500 ml) vegetable broth

1 shallot, minced

10½ oz (300 g) lean ground beef

3 tbsps grated Parmesan cheese

salt and pepper, **5** hazelnuts, minced

2 tbsps breadcrumbs

1 egg, beaten, peanut oil

Heat 2 tablespoons olive oil and sauté the onion until soft. Add the rice and toast, stirring frequently, for a few minutes. Add the saffron and vegetable broth and let cook for 18 minutes. Remove from the heat and let cool. Meanwhile heat 1 tablespoon olive oil and sauté the shallot. Mix together the ground beef, 1 tablespoon olive oil, Parmesan, salt and pepper, then add the mixture to the shallot. Season with salt and pepper and cook for 5 minutes over medium heat.
Take 1 spoonful of rice and flatten it in the palm of the hand. Place a teaspoon of the beef mixture in the middle and then close the rice over it, turning between the hands to make a ball. Let the arancini rest in the refrigerator for 10 minutes. Mix together the hazelnuts and breadcrumbs. Dip the arancini in the beaten egg and then quickly roll them in the breadcrumb mixture.
Heat the peanut oil and fry the arancini. Serve very hot.

The arancini can also be baked in the oven, as long as they are turned frequently so they cook evenly. Brush them with olive oil before baking.

Preparation time **25 minutes**
Cooking time **35 minutes**
Level **easy**

turbot and mozzarella
cannoli with endive

Ingredients for 4 servings

Cannoli:

4 turbot fillets

1 roll of puff pastry

1 braided mozzarella, cut into strips

salt and pepper

Endive:

6 tbsps extra-virgin olive oil

2 heads Belgian endive, sliced

1 tbsp pine nuts, **1** tbsp raisins

1/3 cup (80 ml) white wine

1/2 cup (120 ml) vegetable broth

salt and pepper

Preheat the oven to 400°F (200°C or Gas Mark 6).
Cut the turbot fillets in half. Cut the puff pastry into
8 squares and place a piece of turbot on each square.
Top each piece with some mozzarella strips and season
with salt and pepper. Roll up the pastry, pressing around
the edges to seal. Season with salt.
Bake the cannoli for about 20 minutes. Meanwhile heat
the olive oil and sauté the endive, pine nuts and raisins.
Add the white wine and continue cooking, adding vegetable
broth as the liquid evaporates, until the endive is tender.
Season with salt and pepper.
Serve the cannoli over a bed of sautéed endive.

78

Mozzarella is one of the best-known
Italian cheeses around the world. It can be
made from cow's milk or buffalo's milk
(mozzarella di bufala). Fiordilatte is a kind
of mozzarella made from cow's milk.

Preparation time **35 minutes**
Cooking time **40 minutes**
Level **easy**

mango and herbed goat's cheese rolls

Ingredients for 4 servings

Rolls:

5½ oz (150 g) fresh ricotta

7 oz (200 g) goat's cheese

1 tsp orange-flower honey

salt and pepper

1 bunch chives, minced

1 mango

Garnish:

1 tbsp extra-virgin olive oil

4 slices prosciutto, julienned

Pass the ricotta through a sieve and place in a bowl with the goat's cheese, honey, salt and pepper. Add most of the chives, reserving a few for garnish, and stir the mixture with a wooden spoon until smooth and creamy. Transfer to a pastry bag with a smooth tip. Peel the mango with a paring knife or a vegetable peeler. Slice the mango into thin slices using a mandolin. Lay the slices out on a tray. Pipe a line of the ricotta mixture along the edge of each mango slice. Roll up the slices and sprinkle the ends with some of the remaining chives. Heat the olive oil in a non-stick frying pan and sauté the prosciutto strips until crispy. Sprinkle the prosciutto over the rolls and serve.

The mango has ancient Asian origins. There are over 2,000 different kinds, which are usually divided into two categories: Indian, which are rounder, and Indo-Chinese, which are longer and flatter.

Preparation time **15 minutes**
Cooking time **5 minutes**
Level **easy**

vegetable burritos

Ingredients for 4 servings
Burritos:

1½ cups plus **1½** tbsps (7 oz or 200 g) all-purpose flour

1 tsp active dry yeast, salt

7 tbsps warm water

Filling:

3 tbsps extra-virgin olive oil

1 small onion, thinly sliced

1 cup (9 oz or 250 g) cooked cranberry (borlotti) beans

1/2 cup (5 oz or 140 g) canned sweet corn, drained

1½ cups (3½ oz or 100 g) thinly sliced mushrooms

1 bell pepper, julienned, **1** tomato, diced

1 small zucchini, diced

2 lettuce leaves, shredded

salt and pepper

The best beans are dried, but they need to be pre-soaked before cooking.

Mix together the flour, yeast and a pinch of salt. Add the warm water, mix well, and let rest for 15 minutes. Divide the dough into 4 equal portions and roll them out on a floured work surface with a rolling pin. Cook the tortillas in a non-stick pan over low heat, then set aside and keep warm. Heat the olive oil in a frying pan and brown the onion. Add the beans, sweet corn, mushrooms, bell pepper, tomato, zucchini and lettuce. Season with salt and pepper and cook over low heat for about 10 minutes. Reheat the tortillas if they have become cold. Arrange some of the vegetable mixture in the center of each one, then roll up. Serve hot. The burritos can be accompanied by pureed beans or guacamole, if desired.

Preparation time **30 minutes**
Cooking time **30 minutes**
Level **easy**

shrimp crackers with dipping sauce

Ingredients for 4 servings

Dipping sauce:

2 tbsps sunflower oil

1 white onion, thinly sliced

1 red bell pepper

1 hot red chili pepper

2 tbsps rice vinegar, **2** tbsps sugar

1½ cups (350 ml) water, salt

1/2 tsp cornstarch

Shrimp crackers:

1 package shrimp crackers

peanut oil

Heat the sunflower oil in a saucepan and sauté the onion gently until soft. Peel the bell pepper with a vegetable peeler and cut into thin strips.

Remove the seeds from the chili pepper, cut off the tip and wash the rest with a little vinegar. Mince the chili and add to the onions with the bell pepper strips. Sprinkle over the sugar and add the vinegar. Let evaporate, then continue cooking, adding the water. Season with salt and continue to simmer until the bell pepper is soft and there is still some liquid left. Puree in a food processor or with an immersion blender. Return briefly to the heat and stir in the cornstarch. Heat the peanut oil and fry the shrimp crackers for just a few seconds, until they puff up and become crunchy. Do not let them change color.

Drain and serve with the dipping sauce.

Shrimp crackers can be found in specialty Asian stores, either frozen or preserved in protective packaging.

Preparation time **15 minutes**

Cooking time **5 minutes**

Level **easy**

mini crab spring rolls

Ingredients for 4 servings
Rolls:

9 oz (250 g) plain crab meat, drained salt

chervil or parsley, minced

1 tbsp soy sauce

8 sheets of briq dough or won-ton wrappers

1 zucchini, julienned

1 celery heart, strings removed and julienned

2 carrots, peeled and julienned

1 spring onion, julienned

sunflower oil

Mix together the crab meat, a pinch of salt, some minced chervil or parsley and the soy sauce. Roll out the briq dough, if using, and cut out 2-inch by-2-inch (5 cm by 5 cm) squares, or lay out the won-ton wrappers.

Place a few strips of the different vegetables (zucchini, celery, carrots and spring onion) at the base of each square, and then top with a line of crab meat, crumbled with the fingertips. Fold the sides of the square in and then roll up, with the vegetables and crab in the center.

Brush a little water on the edges and press to seal.

Let sit for a few minutes to dry, then season with salt.

Heat the sunflower oil until very hot and fry the spring rolls, then drain on paper towels.

The spring rolls can be served with a dipping sauce such as sweet chile, horseradish or soy.

Preparation time **20 minutes**
Cooking time **10 minutes**
Level **easy**

crunchy panko shrimp

Ingredients for 4 servings
Shrimp:

32 shrimp

3/4 cup (3½ oz or 100 g)
all-purpose flour

1/3 cup (2 oz or 50 g) rice flour

3 eggs

salt

7 oz (200 g) panko (Japanese
breadcrumbs)

sunflower oil

Shell the shrimp, leaving the end part of the tail attached.
Remove the black vein with a toothpick.
Sift the all-purpose flour and rice flour together.
Beat the eggs in a bowl with a little salt (optionally they
can be seasoned with some dried spices or finely chopped
fresh herbs). Holding the shrimp by the tail, dip them one
at a time first in the flours, then the egg, then the flours
and finally the egg again, tapping to remove any excess.
Dip in the panko and press well so that it sticks.
Lay the dipped shrimp on a tray.
Heat the oil until hot then fry the shrimp until golden.
Drain on paper towels and lightly salt, then serve
immediately while still hot and crispy.

Crispier and airier, the small
white flakes of panko are
quite different from regular,
denser breadcrumbs.

Preparation time **10 minutes**
Cooking time **5 minutes**
Level **easy**

Finger Food

vegetarian spring rolls

Ingredients for 4 servings
Rolls:

1 tbsp peanut oil

1 onion, thinly sliced

1 cup (5½ oz or 150 g) peas

salt

8 frozen won-ton wrappers (or
pre-soaked dried rice paper)

3 carrots, peeled and julienned

2 celery stalks, strings removed
and julienned

4-5 asparagus stalks, peeled
and julienned

sunflower oil

Heat the peanut oil and sauté the onion over high
heat for 5 minutes.
Blanch the peas in boiling salted water, then drain
and immerse in ice water to stop the cooking process.
Lay out the wrappers or rice paper and cut in half to make
rectangles. Place some carrots, celery, peas, asparagus
and sautéed onion along one of the longer edges.
Fold in the sides, then roll up the vegetables, brushing
a little water on the edge and pressing well to seal.
Heat the sunflower oil in a frying pan or wok and fry
the spring rolls until golden.
Drain on paper towels, salt lightly and serve.

The spring rolls can be
served with soy sauce or
another dipping sauce.

Preparation time **10 minutes**
Cooking time **15 minutes**
Level **easy**

vegetable omelet with mustard sprouts

Ingredients for 4 servings

Omelet:

1/2 red bell pepper

1/2 cup (2 oz or 60 g) spring peas

3 eggs, salt

1 tbsp heavy cream

Garnish:

mâche (lamb's lettuce)

mustard sprouts

extra-virgin olive oil, salt and pepper

Roast the bell pepper under the grill, on a cast-iron grill pan or in a hot oven. Wrap it in plastic wrap and let steam for 10 minutes before peeling and cutting into thin strips. Blanch the spring peas, then immerse them in ice water to keep their color.
Beat the eggs with a pinch of salt and the cream, then stir in the pepper strips and peas. Heat a non-stick pan and cook the omelet. Toss the mâche and mustard sprouts with the oil, salt and pepper.
Serve with the omelet.

Fresh sprouts can always be on hand with a home germinator. This simple piece of equipment is available at natural-food stores. Seeds are laid out on the various levels, and must be regularly watered through the hole in the middle of the lid.

Preparation time **30 minutes**
Cooking time **10 minutes**
Level **easy**

red cabbage fritters with béchamel

Ingredients for 4 servings

Fritters:

2 cups (9 oz or 250 g) all-purpose flour

salt, **1** tbsp extra-virgin olive oil

7 tbsps sparkling water, sunflower oil

Filling:

4 tbsps extra-virgin olive oil

1 onion, thinly sliced

1/2 red cabbage, finely sliced

1/2 cup (120 ml) white wine

1 tbsp vinegar, salt and pepper

Béchamel:

2 tbsps (1 oz or 30 g) butter

2 tsps cornstarch

1¼ cups (300 ml) milk

nutmeg, grated

salt and pepper

For a lighter sauce, replace the milk in the béchamel with soy milk.

Mix together the flour, salt, olive oil and sparkling water to obtain a soft and elastic dough. Wrap in plastic wrap and refrigerate for 20 minutes.

Heat the oil for the filling and sauté the onion and red cabbage. Add the white wine and vinegar and let stew for 10 minutes. Season with salt and pepper.

Roll out the dough and cut into triangles.

Place a little filling on half of the triangles and then cover with the other half. Press down around the edges to seal,

Melt the butter in a small saucepan and stir in the cornstarch. Add the milk and bring to a boil, stirring frequently. Simmer for 5 minutes, then add a grating of nutmeg and salt and pepper.

Heat the sunflower oil until hot then fry the fritters. Serve immediately with the béchamel.

Preparation time **1 hour**
Cooking time **25 minutes**
Level **medium**

chickpea and shrimp croquettes

Ingredients for 4 servings

Croquettes:

2 tablespoons extra-virgin olive oil

1 shallot, minced

2/3 cup (5½ oz or 150 g) drained, canned chickpeas

thyme leaves, **1** egg

salt and pepper

20 small shrimp, partially peeled leaving the tail attached

3/4 cup (3½ oz or 100 g) breadcrumbs

sunflower oil

Heat the olive oil in a large frying pan, add the shallot and sauté. Add the chickpeas and thyme.
Let cook for 5 minutes. Puree the mixture using a food processor or immersion blender. When the puree is cool add the egg, salt and pepper and mix well.
Add the shrimp to the chickpea puree and toss to coat. Pour the breadcrumbs onto a large plate, and roll each shrimp in breadcrumbs to coat.
Heat the sunflower oil in a large frying pan and fry the shrimp. As soon as they are golden-brown drain them with a slotted spoon and dry on paper towels, then serve immediately.

Extra flavor can be added to the breading by toasting some sesame seeds in a non-stick pan, grinding them up and then adding them to the breadcrumbs.

Preparation time **15 minutes**
Cooking time **15 minutes**
Level **easy**

Finger Food

lettuce and grouper rolls

Ingredients for 4 servings

Rolls:

10½ oz (300 g) grouper fillet, **1** orange

3 tbsps extra-virgin olive oil

1 garlic clove, smashed

5-6 black olives, pitted and roughly chopped

salt and pepper, parsley, minced

1 head lettuce, **2** tomatoes

extra-virgin olive oil

salt and pepper

4 slices white sandwich bread, butter

Remove any bones from the grouper fillet and cut into pieces. Squeeze the orange and strain the juice. Heat the oil and garlic in a frying pan and brown the fish for 2 minutes. Add the orange juice, let reduce, then add the olives. Season with salt, pepper and a little parsley. Separate the lettuce leaves, keeping them whole, and blanch in boiling water for 3 seconds. Immerse in ice water, then dry on a clean kitchen towel. Place a small amount of grouper in the middle of each leaf, fold in the outside edges and wrap into rolls. Chop the tomatoes, removing the seeds, and toss with oil, salt and pepper. Toast the bread and spread with butter. Serve the lettuce rolls on the toast, topped with a few pieces of tomato.

Preparation time **20 minutes**
Cooking time **5 minutes**
Level **easy**

crispy cheese rolls

Ingredients for 4 servings
Sauce:

2 tbsps extra-virgin olive oil

1¼ cups (5½ oz or 150 g) minced celery, carrot and onion

1¼ cups (9 oz or 250 g) tomato puree

basil leaves, salt and pepper

Rolls:

2 sheets phyllo dough

12½ oz (350 g) mild provola cheese, cut into thick strips

1 egg, beaten, sunflower oil

Heat the olive oil in a small saucepan and sauté the minced celery, carrot and onion until soft.
Add the tomato puree, a little hot water and the basil.
Simmer for 15 minutes then adjust salt and pepper.
Meanwhile cut the phyllo dough into rectangles.
Wrap each strip of cheese in a piece of phyllo, brushing the edges with beaten egg and pinching the ends closed.
Heat abundant sunflower oil and fry the cheese rolls until golden. Drain on paper towels.
Serve the crispy cheese rolls with the tomato sauce.

Provola is a stretched-curd cheese, very similar to mozzarella but with a more compact rind. It can be found both fresh and smoked. When smoked it is usually tied with a cord called a sparto.

Preparation time **20 minutes**
Cooking time **25 minutes**
Level **easy**

figs wrapped in finocchiona

Ingredients for 4 servings

Figs:

6 ripe green figs

12 very thin slices finocchiona

Trim the figs, removing the stalk, the base and any imperfections on the skin.
Halve the figs and wrap each half in a slice of finocchiona, curling over any excess (see photo on right).
Fix with toothpicks or decorated skewers and refrigerate until serving.

102

Finocchiona is a Tuscan cured meat named after the fennel seeds (semi di finocchio) added to the pork, giving a very particular flavor to the finished salami. It is excellent with fresh fava beans.

Preparation time **5 minutes**
Level **easy**

eggplant-wrapped foie gras

Ingredients for 4 servings
Foie Gras:

1 firm eggplant

1 tbsp powdered sugar

salt and pepper

7 oz (200 g) foie gras avec
morceaux, cubed

1/3 cup (2 oz or 50 g) peeled,
unsalted pistachios

1/2 tsp clear honey

Slice the eggplant into very thin rounds and place them on a microwave-proof plate lined with parchment paper. Sprinkle them lightly with powdered sugar, using sifter, then microwave them at maximum power for 90 seconds, until the slices are lightly colored.
Let them cool for 2 minutes then remove from the paper. Season with salt and pepper.
Place a cube of foie gras in the center of each eggplant slice and carefully fold in the sides around the cube, creating a kind of flower.
Mince the pistachios in a food processor.
Sprinkle the rolls with ground pistachios and drizzle with a little honey.

Foie gras avec morceaux is goose foie gras which has been cut into pieces, seasoned and cooked sous-vide.

Preparation time **10 minutes**
Cooking time **2 minutes**
Level **easy**

savory fontina and prosciutto tart

Ingredients for 4 servings

Dough:

2¼ tsp active dry yeast

1 cup plus 3 tbsps (5½ oz or 150 g) whole-wheat flour

2¾ cups (12½ oz or 350 g) all-purpose flour

1 tbsp honey, **2** tsps salt

4 tbsps sunflower oil or extra-virgin olive oil

1 cup (250 ml) warm milk

Filling:

3½ oz (100 g) ham, diced

3½ oz (100 g) fontina or scamorza cheese, diced

The best fontina is made in the summer, when the cows have been eating fresh grass, and then sold in the winter. Fontina is aged in cool, damp environments for about four months.

Dissolve the yeast in a little water.
On a work surface, mix together the whole-wheat flour, all-purpose flour, honey, salt, oil, warm milk and yeast mixture. Knead for a long time, until a smooth and elastic dough is formed. Shape it into a ball, cut an X on top and let sit, covered, for a couple of hours.
Preheat the oven to 350°F (180°C or Gas Mark 4).
Divide the dough in half and roll the halves out into 2 circles about 2/3-inch (1½ cm) thick.
Line a baking sheet with parchment paper and lay one of the circles on top. Cover with the ham and cheese, then top with the other circle of dough.
Close the edges, pressing down with the fingertips, so the cheese does not ooze out during cooking.
Cut a series of incisions on the top, first one way and then the other, creating a kind of cross-hatching.
Bake for 40 minutes.

Preparation time **25 minutes**
Cooking time **40 minutes**
Level **easy**

mini focaccias with green olive pâté and prosciutto

Ingredients for 4 servings

Focaccias:

1 lb (500 g) pre-risen pizza dough

4 tbsps extra-virgin olive oil

3 tbsps milk

3½ oz (100 g) green olive pâté (tapenade)

7 oz (200 g) prosciutto, thinly sliced

Roll out the dough and cut it into circles about 3 to 4 inches (8-10 cm) in diameter. Arrange them on an oiled baking sheet. Let them rise for 20 minutes in a warm place.
Preheat the oven to 425°F (220°C or Gas Mark 7).
Mix together the milk and 2 tablespoons olive oil. Brush the foccacias with the mixture. Bake for 10 minutes. Remove from the oven and cover with a clean kitchen towel. Let cool. Halve the foccacias and fill them with the green olive pâté and the prosciutto. Reclose and serve.

The green olive pâté can be replaced by artichoke or asparagus pâté.

Preparation time **20 minutes**
Cooking time **10 minutes**
Level **easy**

mini panini with truffled crescenza

Ingredients for 4 servings
Panini:

1 black truffle

5½ oz (150 g) crescenza cheese

salt and pepper

2 tbsps truffle oil

8 small, soft butter rolls

8 slices prosciutto

1 firm, fresh porcini mushroom,
thinly sliced

Clean the truffle well with a small brush or a dry cloth and slice it thinly, then mince it. Beat the crescenza with a little salt, pepper and the truffle oil until creamy, then stir in the minced truffle. Halve the rolls and spread them with the crescenza mixture. Top with a slice of prosciutto and a few slices of porcini mushroom.
Close the rolls and press down lightly.
Serve the panini as a snack or paired with pre-dinner drinks.

The truffle, a subterranean ascomycetus fungus, comes in several varieties, from the most expensive and rarest white Alba truffles to the black ones from Norcia and Aqualagna, as well as others. They can be frozen with quite good results.

Preparation time **20 minutes**
Level **easy**

squash cubes on parmesan cream

Ingredients for 4 servings

Squash:

1/2 green-skinned winter squash, such as Kabocha

salt and pepper

1 tbsp extra-virgin olive oil

Parmesan cream:

3½ oz (100 g) Parmesan cheese

1 pinch saffron

Garnish:

4 thin slices prosciutto

Preheat the oven to 350°F (180°C or Gas Mark 4).
Peel the squash and cut the flesh into equal-sized cubes.
Steam them for 6 minutes, until still quite firm,
then toss with a little salt, pepper and the olive oil.
Grate the Parmesan cheese into a small bowl.
Add the saffron and then pour in a little boiling water
while whisking with a small whisk.
Continue whisking until smooth and creamy.
Brown the prosciutto slices in a non-stick frying pan
and then dry them out in the oven for 3 minutes. Pat dry
with paper towels and let cool, then chop them finely.
Place each squash cube on top of a spoonful of Parmesan
cream, and sprinkle with the prosciutto bits.

Squash used to be an Italian street food, sold roasted by hawkers to be eaten while walking. Meanwhile the toasted and salted seeds were a kind of predecessor to popcorn.

Preparation time **20 minutes**
Cooking time **10 minutes**
Level **easy**

crunchy carrot and leek fritters

Ingredients for 4 servings
Fritters:

6 carrots, peeled and julienned

1 leek, julienned

3/4 cup (3½ oz or 100 g)
all-purpose flour

1 cup (5½ oz or 150 g) rice flour

2 tbsps finely ground semolina

7 tbsps very cold sparkling water

sunflower oil

salt and pepper

Place the julienned carrots and leek in a bowl of cold water and refrigerate for 30 minutes. Drain and dry carefully. Mix together the all-purpose flour, rice flour and semolina with the cold sparkling water to make a batter.

Stir the carrots and leek into the batter.

Heat the sunflower oil until very hot, then fry spoonfuls of the batter until golden, working in batches.

Drain on paper towels, sprinkle with salt and pepper and serve immediately.

For a different flavor, replace the carrots with 7 oz (200 g) pumpkin flesh and add a grating of nutmeg to the batter.

Preparation time **15 minutes**
Cooking time **5 minutes**
Level **easy**

cheese wafers with cauliflower cream

Ingredients for 4 servings
Cream:
4 cups (1 l) light vegetable broth
1/2 cauliflower, cut into florets
1 tbsp extra-virgin olive oil
2 thyme sprigs, leaves only, salt
Wafers:
9 oz (250 g) puff pastry, salt
3 tbsps extra-virgin olive oil
1 tbsp grated Parmesan cheese
sesame seeds

Preheat the oven to 400°F (200°C or Gas Mark 6).
Bring the vegetable broth to a boil in a saucepan and then add the cauliflower. Cook until very tender, then drain.
Let cool then place in a food processor or blender with 1 tablespoon of olive oil, the thyme leaves and a little salt, and puree until smooth.
Roll the puff pastry out until thin. Sprinkle with salt and brush with a little oil. Poke holes in the surface with a fork and sprinkle over the Parmesan and sesame seeds.
Cut the dough into many little triangles and place them on a baking sheet lined with waxed paper.
Bake for 10 minutes, until golden-brown. Serve the cold cauliflower cream with the warm cheese wafers.

Food processors and blenders are useful kitchen tools for mincing, chopping, blending and pureeing. Immersion or hand-held blenders can be placed directly into the food container.

Preparation time **20 minutes**
Cooking time **30 minutes**
Level **easy**

baby squid tempura

Ingredients for 4 servings

Tempura:

3/4 cup (3½ oz or 100 g)
all-purpose flour

very cold sparkling water

sunflower oil

12½ oz (350 g) baby squid, cleaned

2 carrots, julienned

4-5 asparagus spears, peeled
and sliced lengthways

1 zucchini, sliced lengthways

salt and pepper

Mix the flour with enough cold sparkling water to make a thin batter. Heat the sunflower oil until very hot. Dip the vegetables and squid in the batter and fry separately. Drain on paper towels and season with salt and pepper to taste.

Frying oil can be used just twice if heated to high temperatures, or four times if used only at low to medium temperatures.

Preparation time **20 minutes**
Cooking time **20 minutes**
Level **easy**

freshwater fish fry with vegetables

Ingredients for 4 servings

Fish:

10½ oz (300 g) tiny whitefish or other whitebait

3/4 cup (3½ oz or 100 g) all-purpose flour

2 tbsps semolina flour

sparkling water

sunflower oil

2 carrots, peeled and julienned

2 zucchini, julienned, salt

Whitefish, Coregonus lavaretus, is a freshwater fish which lives deep at the bottom of large lakes and can also be farmed. A delicious fish, it can be prepared in many ways. In Umbria it is often roasted, while in Lombardy it is seasoned with sage. In this recipe the whitefish can be replaced by any other whitebait, tiny fish which can be eaten whole.

Wash the fish several times under cold running water and let drain in a strainer. Mix together the all-purpose flour and semolina in a bowl. Pour in the sparkling water in a thin stream, whisking constantly, to obtain a liquid batter. Heat the oil in a wide frying pan.
First dip the vegetables in the batter and then fry in the hot oil. Drain on paper towels.
Repeat with the fish. Salt and serve hot and crunchy.

Preparation time **10 minutes**
Cooking time **10 minutes**
Level **easy**

pike in a potato crust with thyme

Ingredients for 4 servings
Pike:

1 lb (500 g) pike fillets

7 tbsps extra-virgin olive oil

salt and pepper

thyme leaves

2 firm yellow-fleshed potatoes

1 bunch mixed salad leaves

Descale and debone the pike fillets, leaving the skin intact. Lay on a tray and cover with 4 tablespoons olive oil, salt, pepper and thyme leaves and let marinate. Peel the potatoes and grate them with a coarse grater. Season the grated potatoes with salt and pepper.
Press the potatoes on top of the fillets, on the side without skin, then cut the fillets into diamond shapes.
Tear the salad leaves into small pieces and dress with 2 tablespoons olive oil, salt and pepper. Divide between serving plates. Heat the remaining tablespoon of olive oil in a non-stick frying pan and sauté the fish fillets, starting with the potato side. Turn over and finish cooking. Serve the fish with the salad.

If pike cannot be found, trout fillets can also be used for this recipe. The fish can also be cooked in the oven, taking care to turn it frequently so it cooks evenly.

Preparation time **15 minutes**
Cooking time **10 minutes**
Level **easy**

tempura oysters with ginger and lemon zabaglione

Ingredients for 4 servings

Oysters:

12 oysters, **3/4** cup (3½ oz or 100 g) all-purpose flour

3/4 cup (3½ oz or 100 g) rice flour

2½ tbsps finely ground semolina flour

1 tsp active dry yeast

very cold sparkling water, sunflower oil

Zabaglione:

1 egg yolk, **1** tbsp liquid from oysters

4 tsps lemon juice

1 pinch ground ginger, salt and pepper

Garnish:

fried basil leaves (optional)

powdered saffron (optional)

It has been scientifically proven that oysters, along with other shellfish, are actually aphrodisiacs. They contain a substance that encourages the production of a hormone which stimulates sexual activity.

Shell the oysters and lay to dry on paper towels. Reserve 1 tablespoon of the liquid inside the shells for the zabaglione. Sift together the all-purpose flour and rice flour. Add the semolina and yeast. Whisk in enough cold sparkling water to make a smooth, dense batter.

Heat the sunflower oil in a non-stick pan.

Dip the oysters in the batter then fry them in the hot oil and drain on paper towels.

Meanwhile whisk the egg yolk with the reserved oyster liquid, lemon juice and ginger and place over a double boiler. Continue whisking for 3 minutes until the mixture is fluffy. Adjust salt and pepper.

Serve the crunchy fried oysters with the zabaglione. Garnish with fried basil leaves and a pinch of powdered saffron, if desired.

Preparation time **20 minutes**
Cooking time **5 minutes**
Level **medium**

oysters with pepper and lemon

Ingredients for 4 servings

Oysters:

16 large oysters

1 juicy lemon

freshly ground black pepper

Open the oysters using a shucking tool, and leave the oyster itself in the deeper part of the shell. Place them on a tray of chopped ice. Just before serving, squeeze a few drops of lemon juice over each oyster and sprinkle with a little freshly ground pepper.

This classic preparation is still the best way to eat oysters, as the light seasoning does not hide the full taste of the oysters.

Preparation time **5 minutes**
Level **easy**

oysters with yogurt sauce

Ingredients for 4 servings

Oysters:

8 very fresh oysters

Sauce:

white horseradish

1 tsp lemon juice

1 tsp light extra-virgin olive oil

1/2 cup (120 ml) plain low-fat yogurt

white pepper

Grate the white horseradish and squeeze it out to obtain 1/2 teaspoon of horseradish juice. Mix together the lemon juice, horseradish juice, olive oil and yogurt. Whisk for a long time to obtain a light and creamy mixture. Open the oysters with a shucking tool.
Place each oyster in a tablespoon, bent for serving (see photo on the right). Arrange the oyster spoons on serving plates, on chopped ice if desired. Sprinkle the yogurt sauce with white pepper and serve with the oysters.

Horseradish can be cultivated, but it also grows wild in damp places and along shady paths around Europe. If the root is used, it should be harvested at the beginning of the autumn from plants at least three years old.

Preparation time **10 minutes**
Level **easy**

phyllo crisps with caviar

Ingredients for 4 servings

Crisps:

2 sheets phyllo dough

3 tbsps (1½ oz or 40 g) melted butter

salt

Topping:

3½ tbsps low-fat yogurt

3 drops lemon juice

2 drops Worcestershire sauce

salt

3 tbsps caviar

Preheat the oven to 350°F (180°C or Gas Mark 4).
Roll out the phyllo dough and brush with melted butter.
Lightly salt and cut out many small strips using a rolling cutter or a sharp knife. Bake for 3 minutes, then let cool.
Mix together the yogurt, lemon juice and Worcestershire sauce, seasoning with salt to taste.
Place a small amount of sauce on each crisp and top with caviar. Serve immediately.

For a really stunning presentation, cook the phyllo strips over a cylindrical mold to make a curved shape like a long-handled spoon.

Preparation time **10 minutes**
Cooking time **3 minutes**
Level **easy**

bean and chickpea squares
with pistachios

Ingredients for 4 servings
Bean:

3/4 cup (5½ oz or 150 g) dried
cranberry (borlotti) beans

3/4 cup (5½ oz or 150 g)
dried chickpeas

2 garlic cloves, smashed

2 tomatoes, sage and thyme

1/2 dried red chili pepper, halved

3 tbsps heavy cream

2 tbsps extra-virgin olive oil

salt and pepper, **2** eggs

1⅓ cups (5½ oz or 160 g) pistachios,
roughly chopped

Preheat the oven to 375°F (190°C or Gas Mark 5).
Soak the beans and chickpeas separately in cold
water overnight. Cook them separately in two pressure
cookers, each with 1 garlic clove, 1 tomato, sage, thyme
and 1/4 chili pepper until soft, or use regular saucepans
(cooking time will be longer). Let the beans and chickpeas
cool and drain them from their cooking liquid.
Transfer the beans to a food processor with 1½ tablespoons
cream, a little oil, salt, pepper and 1 egg. Puree to
a cream and then transfer to a buttered and floured
square or rectangular cake tin. Level off with a spatula.
Repeat with the chickpeas and remaining cream, oil,
salt, pepper and egg. Pour the mixture over the beans
and level off.
Sprinkle with pistachios. Bake for 25 minutes.
Let cool before cutting into squares and serving.

If the puree is too thick, add a little of
the cooking liquid from the beans and
chickpeas. Make sure not to add the egg
to the beans and chickpeas while still
warm, or it will scramble.

Preparation time **15 minutes**
Cooking time **55 minutes**
Level **easy**

giant chickpea and goat's cheese croquettes

Ingredients for 4 servings
Croquettes:

1 cup (7 oz or 200 g) dried chickpeas
2 tbsps extra-virgin olive oil
1 shallot, minced
6 sage leaves, roughly chopped
salt and pepper, **1/2** cup (120 ml) milk
2 slices country-style bread, **2** eggs
3½ oz (100 g) fresh,
mild goat's milk cheese

breadcrumbs, sunflower oil

Soak the chickpeas overnight, then boil until tender. Heat the oil in a saucepan and sauté the shallot until translucent. Add the chickpeas and sage leaves and continue cooking until the chickpeas are almost falling apart, adding hot water if necessary. Season with salt and pepper to taste.
Soak the bread in the milk until soft, then drain and squeeze out excess liquid. Puree the chickpeas, soaked bread and 1 egg in a food processor, then stir in the goat's cheese. Refrigerate the mixture until firm, adding breadcrumbs if necessary. Beat the remaining egg. Form the chickpea mixture into large cylindrical croquettes. Dip them first in beaten egg and then in breadcrumbs. Heat the sunflower oil until hot and fry the croquettes. Drain on paper towels and salt.
Serve immediately; they should be crunchy outside and melting inside.

For a more delicate flavor, replace the goat's milk cheese with a fresh, soft cow's milk cheese, such as stracchino.

Preparation time **20 minutes**
Cooking time **1 hour**
Level **easy**

sesame, pumpkin and sunflower seed croquettes

Ingredients for 4 servings

Croquettes:

3/4 tsp active dry yeast

1/2 cup (130 ml) warm water

salt

1½ cups plus 1½ tbsps (7 oz or 200 g) all-purpose flour

1 tbsp sesame seeds

1 tbsp black sesame seeds

1 tbsp sunflower seeds, chopped

1 tbsp shelled pumpkin seeds, chopped

sunflower oil

Dissolve the yeast in the warm water in a large mixing bowl and add a little salt. Add the flour and all the seeds and mix to obtain an elastic batter.
Leave to rise in a dry place for about an hour.
Heat the sunflower oil in a wide frying pan.
As soon as it is very hot, starting frying small quantities of the batter, using 2 tablespoons to form the portions.
Turn with a slotted spoon so they cook evenly and drain when golden and crunchy.

To make portioning the batter easier, dip the tablespoons into cold water between use to remove any excess batter.

Preparation time **10 minutes**
Cooking time **5 minutes**
Level **easy**

miniature savory croissants

Ingredients for 4 servings
Croissants:

1 lb (500 g) puff pastry
3½ oz (100 g) prosciutto, cubed
3½ oz (100 g) ham, cubed
3½ oz (100 g) salami, cubed
5½ oz (150 g) frankfurter, chopped
1 egg, lightly beaten
3 tbsps (1 oz or 30 g) sesame seeds

Preheat the oven to 400°F (200°C or Gas Mark 6).
Roll out the puff pastry into a rectangle 1/5-inch (1/2 cm) thick. Cut out triangles with a base about 4 inches (10 cm) long and about 6 inches (15 cm) high.
Place one piece of meat at the base of each triangle and roll up the pastry. Curve the ends around to form a small croissant. Continue making croissants, alternating different kinds of meat, until they are all finished.
Place the rolls on a baking sheet lined with parchment paper and brush them with the beaten egg. Sprinkle with sesame seeds and bake for up to 10 minutes.
Let cool slightly and serve.

Try filling the miniature croissants with other combinations such as speck and Brie; pancetta and creamy Gorgonzola; or prosciutto, arugula and stracchino cheese.

Preparation time **20 minutes**
Cooking time **10 minutes**
Level **easy**

Finger Food

potato blinis with smoked salmon

Ingredients for 6 servings
Blinis:

1 small potato (about 5½ oz or 150 g)

3/4 cup (3½ oz or 100 g)
all-purpose flour

3/4 cup (3½ oz or 100 g)
buckwheat flour

2 eggs, **1** tsp active dry yeast

1 tsp sugar, salt and pepper

2/3 cup (150 ml) milk

3½ tbsps (2 oz or 50 g) melted butter

3 tbsps extra-virgin olive oil

1 shallot, sliced, **2** fennel bulbs, chopped

1/2 cup (120 ml) water

9 oz (250 g) smoked salmon

dill (optional)

Blinis are one of the basics of popular Russian cooking, similar to French crêpes, Mexican tortillas and Italian crespelle.

Boil, peel and mash the potato.
Mix together the mashed potato, all-purpose flour, buckwheat flour, eggs, yeast, sugar and a pinch of salt.
Stir in the milk and melted butter.
Mix well to combine, then let sit for 20 minutes.
Heat a small non-stick frying pan and brush it with oil. Pour in 1 ladleful of the potato batter and spread it out slightly. When the bottom is golden, turn over and continue cooking. When cooked on both sides, remove from the pan and keep warm. Continue making blinis until the batter is finished. Heat a little olive oil and sauté the shallot. Add the fennel, salt and water and continue cooking, covered, for 15-20 minutes. Puree the mixture, adjust salt and pepper, cover and keep warm.
Compose plates by alternating a spoonful of fennel puree, a blini, a slice of smoked salmon, another blini and another slice of smoked salmon.
Decorate with dill, if desired.

Preparation time **30 minutes**
Cooking time **25 minutes**
Level **easy**

black rice wafers
with shrimp and tomatoes

Ingredients for 4 servings

Wafers:

1/4 cup (2 oz or 50 g) Roma rice

3 cups (1½ l) water

salt and pepper

1/2 tsp nero di seppie (squid ink)

10 medium-small shrimp

2 tomatoes

2 tbsps extra-virgin olive oil

1 dill sprig, minced

Roma rice has long grains, firm and dense, and they can absorb any flavoring while remaining compact and separate.

Preheat the oven to 350°F (180°C or Gas Mark 4). Place the rice in a saucepan and cover with the water. Lightly salt and cook for 25 minutes, adding the nero di seppie halfway through. The rice should be overcooked. Puree with an immersion blender to obtain a sticky cream. Spread a little of the cream on a baking sheet lined with parchment paper with the back of a tablespoon to form a circle. Repeat to make a total of 4 circles and bake for about 12 minutes.
Meanwhile steam the shrimp and shell them. Blanch the tomatoes and peel, deseed and dice. Toss the tomatoes with oil, salt, pepper and dill. Chop the shrimp and add to the tomatoes. Serve the tomato-shrimp mixture on top of the rice wafers.

Preparation time **15 minutes**
Cooking time **30 minutes**
Level **easy**

celery sticks with herbed cheese

Ingredients for 4 servings
Sticks:

3½ oz (100 g) sheep's milk ricotta

5½ oz (150 g) mild goat's milk cheese

3½ oz (100 g) soft, spreadable cheese

1 tbsp minced aromatic herbs
(thyme, basil, chives)

1 tbsp light extra-virgin olive oil

salt and freshly ground black pepper

4 celery stalks

Pass the ricotta through a sieve to remove any lumps and place in a bowl. Add the other cheeses and mix well. Stir in the mixed herbs with a wooden spoon. Continue stirring and pour in the olive oil in a thin stream. Add a pinch of salt and freshly ground black pepper and stir well. Refrigerate the mixture for an hour so the flavors can develop. To serve, place a spoonful of the mixture on each celery stalk and serve immediately. For a more original presentation, use a pastry bag to attractively pipe the cheese mixture.

144

There are different kinds of fresh, spreadable cheese, such as cream cheese and Italian crescenza and stracchino.

Preparation time **15 minutes**
Level **easy**

cod fritters with layered salad

Ingredients for 4 servings

Fritters:

2 cups (500 ml) milk

2 cups (500 ml) water

10½ oz (300 g) salt cod fillet, soaked and peeled

2 tbsps mayonnaise, all-purpose flour

1 egg, beaten, breadcrumbs

sunflower oil

Salad:

selection of salad vegetables (tomatoes, bell peppers, celery, carrots, zucchini, fennel, red onions, radishes, cucumbers), thinly sliced

6 tbsps extra-virgin olive oil, vinegar, salt

Whether fresh or preserved, cod is one of the world's most popular fish. It has a very delicate flavor, and is usually cooked with strong aromatic herbs or spices.

Make layers of the different kinds of vegetables in a terrine dish, dressing each layer with oil, vinegar and salt. Cover with plastic wrap and place a weight on top to press out excess water. Let sit for 30 minutes.

Bring the water and milk to a boil and boil the salt cod. Drain, finely chop and mix with mayonnaise.

Form the cod mixture into quenelles.

Dip them in the flour, then the beaten egg and finally the breadcrumbs.

Heat the sunflower oil and fry the fritters.

Serve the fritters with slices of the layered salad.

Preparation time **10 minutes**
Cooking time **10 minutes**
Level **easy**

prosciutto and melon skewers with thyme

Ingredients for 4 servings

Skewers:

1 firm melon

4 oz (120 g) prosciutto, thinly sliced

fresh thyme, minced

thyme sprigs

Peel the melon and remove the seeds. Using a melon baller, cut out many small balls of melon. Refrigerate.
Remove the excess fat from the prosciutto slices.
Cut the slices into 1/2-inch (1 cm) wide strips.
Wrap the prosciutto strips around the melon balls.
Sprinkle with minced thyme.
Thread the melon balls on toothpicks and serve garnished with thyme sprigs.

For a more original presentation, replace the toothpicks with stalks of lemongrass, available in Asian supermarkets.

Preparation time **10 minutes**
Level **easy**

baked chickpea and oat snacks

Ingredients for 4 servings
Snacks:

1 cup (7 oz or 200 g) dried chickpeas

1 garlic clove

1-inch (2 cm) piece of kombu seaweed

1¼ cups (3½ oz or 100 g) oat flakes

salt, **1** tbsp tahini

1 tbsp minced parsley

2 small spring onions, minced

3/4 cup (3½ oz or 100 g) breadcrumbs

2 tbsps gomasio (sesame salt)

5 tbsps extra-virgin olive oil

Soak the chickpeas overnight in water. Drain and boil in fresh water with the garlic clove and piece of kombu for about 45 minutes.
Preheat the oven to 400°F (200°C or Gas Mark 6).
Drain the chickpeas and puree with the oat flakes, salt and tahini in a food processor. Add the parsley and spring onion. The mixture should be quite soft. Form it into balls a little bigger than a walnut.
Mix together the breadcrumbs and gomasio and then dip the balls in the mixture.
Arrange them on a baking sheet lined with parchment paper and brush them with olive oil.
Bake for 10-12 minutes.
Serve with a crunchy salad, if desired.

Tahini is a puree of sesame seeds, used in Middle Eastern and Greek cooking as a starter. It can be found in specialty markets and bigger supermarkets.

Preparation time **30 minutes**
Cooking time **55 minutes**
Level **easy**

mozzarella and cherry tomato skewers

Ingredients for 4 servings
Skewers:
10 cherry tomatoes
salt
10 mozzarella balls
20 basil leaves
2 tbsps extra-virgin olive oil

Halve the cherry tomatoes and lightly salt.
Drain the mozzarella balls from any liquid and halve them.
Wash the basil leaves in cold water to make them crisp.
Carefully dry them.
Thread the tomatoes, mozzarella and basil on wooden skewers, alternating the ingredients.
Drizzle with olive oil and serve.

The skewers can be made in advance and stored in the refrigerator, over a layer of damp paper towels and covered with plastic wrap, so they do not dry out. Drizzle with oil just before serving.

Preparation time **5 minutes**
Level **easy**

sushi with caviar and basmati rice

Ingredients for 4 servings
Sushi:

3/4 cup (6 oz or 170 g) Basmati rice

salt

1 piece of kombu seaweed
(1 inch or 3 cm), washed

1 tsp sugar

1 tbsp rice vinegar

4 sheets of nori seaweed

2½ tbsps Beluga caviar

Wash the rice several times in a collander under cold water, or leave it to sit for 3-4 minutes in a bowl with cold running water. Drain and place in a small saucepan, and cover with 1½ cups (350 ml) water.
Add a little salt and the kombu.
Bring to a boil and let boil gently for 5 minutes, then cover and continue cooking over low heat until cooked through.
Transfer the rice to a bowl and let cool while stirring with a wooden spoon.
Dissolve the sugar in the rice vinegar and add to the rice. Continue stirring until cooled.
Lay out the sheets of nori and place small amounts of rice on them. Roll up and cut into two cylinders.
Stand upright and top with caviar, then serve.

154

Basmati rice is one of the best-known Asian rices. During cooking Basmati rice absorbs less water than Italian short-grain rices, and so is less sticky. It is ideal for use in pilafs or rice salads.

Preparation time **15 minutes**
Cooking time **15 minutes**
Level **easy**

mini vegetable tarts with a potato crust

Ingredients for 4 servings

Tarts:

2 tbsps extra-virgin olive oil

1/2 onion, minced

1 wedge of pumpkin, peeled and diced

1 carrot, peeled and diced

2 zucchini, green part only, diced

salt and pepper

vegetable broth (optional)

1 tomato, diced, nutmeg, grated

2 small potatoes, peeled and very thinly sliced

2 eggs, **1** tbsp grated Parmesan cheese

Preheat the oven to 375°F (190°C or Gas Mark 5).
Heat the olive oil in a saucepan and sauté the onion until golden. Add the pumpkin, cook for 3 minutes, then add the carrots and zucchini.
Season with salt and pepper and continue cooking, adding a little water or vegetable broth if necessary. Add the tomato when the other vegetables are almost done. When the vegetables are cooked through, sprinkle with a little grated nutmeg and let cool.
Blanch the potato slices in boiling salted water, then drain and use them to line small oiled molds.
Beat the eggs in a bowl with salt and pepper.
Stir in the Parmesan and cooled vegetables.
Fill the potato-lined molds with the vegetable mixture and bake for 15 minutes.
Serve warm.

In Italy nutmeg was once used to make a kind of medicine, known as the aceto dei sette ladri, "the vinegar of the seven thieves." A maceration of spices and herbs, it was used to prepare compresses and to revive people who had fainted.

Preparation time **20 minutes**
Cooking time **30 minutes**
Level **easy**

Finger Food

onion, tomato and feta mezzelune

Ingredients for 4 servings
Dough:

4 cups (1 lb 1½ oz or 500 g)
all-purpose flour
1/2 cup (120 ml) extra-virgin olive oil
juice of **1** lemon
7 tbsps water, **1/2** tsp salt
Filling:

1/2 cup (120 ml) extra-virgin olive oil
2 lb (1 kg) onions, thinly sliced
3 tomatoes, thinly sliced
salt and pepper
3½ oz (100 g) feta cheese, crumbled

Heat the olive oil for the filling and sauté the onions until golden. Add the tomatoes, salt and pepper.
Simmer until the sauce thickens, then add the feta.
Remove from the heat.
Mix together the flour, 1/4 cup (60 ml) olive oil, lemon juice, water and salt to make a dough, then roll out to a thickness of 1/5 inch (1/2 cm).
Cut out circles 4 inches (10 cm) in diameter, and place a spoonful of filling in the center of each one.
Fold the circles over to make half-moons, and press around the edges with a fork to seal.
Heat the remaining olive oil and fry the mezzelune, turning so they become golden-brown on both sides.
Drain on paper towels and serve.

Onions come in many different guises: golden, white, red, purple, large and small, round and flat. Dark purple onions have a very intense flavor, white onions are more delicate, while red Tropea onions are the sweetest. To avoid tears while peeling them, keep them under running water.

Preparation time **5 minutes**
Cooking time **15 minutes**
Level **easy**

spiced beef won-tons

Ingredients for 4 servings
Won-tons:

3½ oz (100 g) ground beef

2 spring onions, minced

1 red chili pepper, deseeded and minced

2 tsps minced galangal

1 garlic clove, minced

zest and juice of **1/2** organic lime

1 tsp minced coriander

1 tbsp soy sauce, **1** egg, separated

salt and pepper, **16** won-ton wrappers

sunflower oil

Mix together the beef, spring onions, chili, galangal and garlic. Stir in the lime zest and juice, coriander, soy sauce, egg yolk, salt and pepper.
Cut each won-ton wrapper into 4 squares. Lay 2 squares on top of each other.
Place a small amount of filling at the bottom and roll up two-thirds of the wrapper. Brush the two ends, left and right, with egg white, and close with the fingers. Separate the two top ends of the roll.
Continue until all the filling and wrappers have been used up. Keep the prepared won-tons under a damp kitchen towel until ready to fry.
Heat abundant sunflower oil in a wok, or a large saucepan, and fry the won-tons until golden.
Drain on paper towels and serve hot.

Galangal is similar to ginger but has a more subtle flavor. The name derives from khalanjian, the Arabic adaptation of the Chinese liang-tiang, meaning "delicate ginger". It is used in Asian cuisines.

Preparation time **15 minutes**
Cooking time **15 minutes**
Level **medium**

tortilla chips with spicy sausage salsa

Ingredients for 4 servings
Tortillas:

2 tbsps extra-virgin olive oil

1 shallot, minced

1 red chili pepper, deseeded and minced

1 large peppered sausage

1 cup (6½ oz or 180 g) chopped tomatoes

salt and pepper, parsley, minced

7 oz (200 g) corn tortilla chips

Heat the olive oil in a saucepan and gently sauté the shallot and chili until soft.
Remove the casing from the sausage and crumble the meat into the saucepan. Raise the heat and brown the meat, breaking it up with a fork.
Add the tomatoes and cook gently over low heat for about 10 minutes. Season with salt and pepper to taste. Stir in the parsley and serve at room temperature, accompanied by the tortilla chips.

Tortillas are an ancient, pre-Colombian food. Corn tortillas are prepared by grinding corn kernels into flour, which is then mixed with water. The dough is formed into balls, flattened out into disks, and cooked over a fire on a rudimentary griddle. The tortillas are then served with different meats, vegetables or sauces.

Preparation time **10 minutes**
Cooking time **10 minutes**
Level **easy**

three-flavored corn rolls

Ingredients for 4 servings
Rolls:

1 cup (4 oz or 125 g) all-purpose flour

2/3 cup (3½ oz or 100 g) finely ground cornmeal

2 tsps active dry yeast, salt

7 tbsps milk, at room temperature

2 tbsps sugar

2 tbsps (1 oz or 30 g) melted butter, at room temperature

1 egg, beaten

1 tbsp poppy seeds

1 tbsp fennel seeds

1 tbsp sesame seeds

Sift together the flour and cornmeal with the yeast and a pinch of salt. Add the milk and sugar and mix together gently. Quickly add the melted butter and continue mixing until it forms a smooth and elastic dough.
Wrap in plastic wrap and refrigerate for 20 minutes.
Preheat the oven to 350°F (180°C or Gas Mark 4).
Form the dough into small balls.
Brush with beaten egg.
Place on baking sheet lined with parchment paper and press down to flatten slightly.
Sprinkle a third with poppy seeds, a third with fennel seeds, and a third with sesame seeds.
Bake for 20 minutes. Serve warm.

The corn rolls could be served with peanut butter, or any other spread or sauce, as desired.

Preparation time **20 minutes**
Cooking time **25 minutes**
Level **easy**

spinach and tofu tortelli

Ingredients for 4 servings

Dough:

1 tsp active dry yeast

1½ cups plus 1½ tbsps (7 oz or 200 g) all-purpose flour

2½ tbsps finely ground cornmeal

3 tbsps sunflower oil

salt, sesame seeds

Filling:

1 tbsp extra-virgin olive oil

9 oz (250 g) spinach

10½ oz (300 g) fresh tofu, diced

1 tsp thyme leaves, parsley, minced

Preheat the oven to 400°F (200°C or Gas Mark 6). Dissolve the yeast in a little hot water and let sit for 10 minutes. Mound the flour and cornmeal together on a work surface and make a well in the center. Pour in the sunflower oil, a little water and the yeast mixture.

Add salt and mix together to form a smooth and elastic dough. Form into a ball.

Heat the olive oil in a saucepan and sauté the spinach. Add the tofu and cook for 10 minutes. Add the thyme and parsley and puree the mixture in a food processor. Roll the dough out with a rolling pin and cut into 4-inch (10 cm) diameter circles.

Place a small ball of the spinach mixture in the center of each one and fold over into a half-moon, pressing around the edges to seal.

Sprinkle with sesame seeds and bake for 15 minutes. Serve at room temperature.

166

Tofu is a Chinese and Japanese specialty, which can be found in most supermarkets and Asian markets. It is sometimes called "soy cheese" because it looks like cheese and is made from soy beans.

Preparation time **30 minutes**
Cooking time **25 minutes**
Level **easy**

tuna and artichoke baguettes

Ingredients for 4 servings
Baguettes:

1 baguette

9 oz (250 g) artichokes in oil

3½ oz (100 g) roasted peppers in oil

5½ oz (150 g) tuna in oil

1 bunch arugula, torn into pieces

3 spring onions, minced

4 anchovy fillets in salt, rinsed

salt and pepper

Slice the baguette horizontally, being careful to leave one side in tact, and open it up like a book. Remove some of the crumb.

Drain the artichokes, peppers and tuna from their oil and mix them together in a bowl with the arugula, spring onions and anchovies.

Salt and pepper the inside of the baguette and fill with the artichoke mixture. Close the baguette and wrap in plastic wrap. Refrigerate for a few hours.

Before serving cut the baguette into 1-inch (2 cm) lengths and arrange in a pyramid on a serving plate.

This quick and easy sandwich makes a great snack and is very convenient because it can be prepared in advance. It is important to wrap the baguette tightly in plastic wrap, and let it rest for a while, so the flavors can meld and the bread can soften.

Preparation time **10 minutes**
Level **easy**

miniature crescenza tarts

Ingredients for 4 servings

Tart shells:

1/2 tsp active dry yeast, honey

1 cup plus 3 tbsps (5½ oz or 150 g) all-purpose flour

2 tbsps sesame oil, **1** tsp salt

Filling:

9 oz (250 g) crescenza cheese

7 Taggiasca olives, minced

zest of **1** organic lemon

1 tbsp extra-virgin olive oil

salt and pepper

Garnish:

15 pitted Taggiasca olives in oil, drained and sliced

Taggiasca olives are small black olives from Liguria with a very distinctive flavor. They make an excellent tapenade, or olive pâté. They can be replaced by other black olives in oil.

Preheat the oven to 375°F (190°C or Gas Mark 5). Place the yeast in a small cup with a drop of honey and mix with warm water until dissolved. Let sit for at least 10 minutes.

Mound the flour on a wooden pastry board and make well in the center. Pour in the sesame oil.

Sprinkle the salt around the edge of the mound.

Pour in the yeast mixture and mix together quickly, then knead for some time to form a smooth dough.

Roll the dough out with a rolling pin and cut out little rounds, using a glass or cookie cutter.

Arrange them on a baking sheet lined with parchment paper and bake for 15 minutes.

Meanwhile beat the crescenza until creamy.

Stir in the olives, lemon zest, oil, salt and pepper.

Fill the tart shells with the crescenza mixture and garnish with slices of olive.

Preparation time **20 minutes**
Cooking time **15 minutes**
Level **easy**

Finger Food

canapés

Finger Foods

salmon canapés

Ingredients for 4 servings

Canapés:

8 slices of bread

7 tbsps (3½ oz or 100 g) butter,
at room temperature

7 oz (200 g) salmon fillet, thinly sliced

dill sprigs

Cut the bread slices into small squares.
Spread with butter.
Lay a slice of salmon on each piece of bread.
Garnish with dill sprigs.

Canapés

174

Both the leaves and seeds of dill can be used in the kitchen. The herb can be used to season soups, sauces and dips, and pairs particularly well with fish as well as cream, yogurt and eggs. Dill seeds are harvested at the end of the summer and the leaves in August. They can be found fresh or dried, but are best fresh.

Preparation time **5 minutes**
Level **easy**

oat bread with buffalo mozzarella, pesto and tomatoes

Ingredients for 4 servings

Bread:

2 tomatoes

8 slices soft oat bread

9 oz (250 g) buffalo's milk mozzarella, thinly sliced

4 tbsps Genoan pesto

Cut an X in the bottom of the tomatoes and blanch in boiling salted water for 1 minute.
Drain and immerse in cold water, then drain again and peel. Slice into 4 wedges and remove the seeds, then dice the flesh.
Lay the mozzarella on the bread slices, covering them well. Drizzle over a little pesto then top with tomatoes. Season with salt and pepper to taste then cut the bread into small shapes. Serve.

Ready-made pesto in a jar can be replaced with home-made pesto, made by pureeing 1 tablespoon toasted pine nuts, 1 bunch basil, 5 tbsps extra-virgin olive oil, a little grated Parmesan cheese and salt in a food processor.

Preparation time **20 minutes**
Cooking time **1 minutes**
Level **easy**

Canapés

monkfish tartare with pink grapefruit

Ingredients for 4 servings
Tartare:

9 oz (250 g) monkfish fillet

zest and juice of **1/2** lemon

salt

black and white pepper

lemon thyme leaves

parsley, minced

6 tbsps light extra-virgin olive oil

1 ripe pink grapefruit

2 slices rye bread

1 garlic clove, halved

For an unusual flavor, replace the lemon juice with raspberry vinegar, and also use the vinegar to dress the grapefruit.

Wash the monkfish well and slice it first into thin slices and then into julienne strips. Place in a bowl.
Whisk together the lemon juice, salt, white pepper, lemon thyme, parsley and a little olive oil.
Pour over the monkfish and refrigerate for 30 minutes.
Meanwhile peel the grapefruit and cut it into segments, removing the white skin and pith.
Cut the bread into 4 circles with a cookie cutter and toast the circles in a non-stick frying pan or a toaster.
Rub with a little garlic.
Top the bread with the monkfish, using a cookie cutter to shape the fish.
Drizzle the grapefruit segments with olive oil and black pepper. Serve with the monkfish tartare, garnished with lemon zest.

Preparation time **15 minutes**
Cooking time **5 minutes**
Level **easy**

shrimp and avocado canapés

Ingredients for 4 servings
Canapés:
1/2 avocado
juice of **1/2** lemon
salt and pink pepper
6½ oz (180 g) small preserved shrimp
3 tbsps Marie Rose sauce
parsley, minced
8 slices whole-wheat bread
parsley sprigs

Peel the avocado, remove the pit and dice the flesh.
Dress with a little lemon juice, salt and pink pepper.
Rinse and drain the shrimp and add to the avocado.
Mix together with the Marie Rose sauce and a little parsley.
Cut the bread into triangles or circles and top with the avocado mixture.
Garnish with parsley sprigs.

Marie Rose sauce can be purchased ready made or prepared at home by mixing together 2 tablespoons mayonnaise, 1/2 tablespoon ketchup and a drop of heavy cream.

Preparation time **20 minutes**
Level **easy**

soft spinach and tomato layers

Ingredients for 4 servings

Soft Layers:

6½ oz (180 g) spinach

salt and pepper

5½ oz (150 g) fresh ricotta

2 tbsps extra-virgin olive oil

nutmeg, grated

6 large slices white sandwich bread

4 tomatoes, thinly sliced

oregano

Blanch the spinach in boiling salted water and drain.
Let cool and squeeze out excess water.
Place in a food processor with the ricotta, olive oil
and a pinch of grated nutmeg.
Puree and adjust salt and pepper to taste.
Spread the spinach puree on 3 slices of bread
and top with the other 3 slices.
Lay the tomato slices on top, slightly overlapping them.
Season with a little salt and oregano.
Cut into squares and arrange on a serving plate or tray.

Spinach, whose healthy properties have been made famous by Popeye, has uncertain origins. Probably from Persia, it arrived in Europe via either the Arabs or the Crusaders. Supposedly the favorite vegetable of Catherine de Medici, it is said that when she married the future king of France she brought her own cooks with her, able to prepare spinach in many different ways.

Canapés

182

Preparation time **15 minutes**
Cooking time **5 minutes**
Level **easy**

corn crackers with smoked salmon and caper sauce

Ingredients for 4 servings

Crackers:

12 crisp corn crackers

3½ oz (100 g) cream cheese

7 oz (200 g) smoked salmon, thinly sliced

Sauce:

2 spring onions, thinly sliced

2 tomatoes, diced

2 tbsps capers

juice of 1 lemon

1 tbsp extra-virgin olive oil

dill, chopped

Garnish:

arugula (optional)

Mix together the spring onions, tomatoes, capers, lemon juice, olive oil and dill.

Spread each cracker with cream cheese and lay some smoked salmon on top.

Finish with the caper sauce and garnish with arugula if desired.

The cream cheese could be replaced by a fresh goat's milk cheese, for a stronger flavor.

Preparation time **10 minutes**
Level **easy**

Canapés

184

salmon, lettuce and olive canapés

Ingredients for 4 servings

Canapés:

1/2 head lettuce

2 tbsps extra-virgin olive oil

1 garlic clove, smashed

salt and pepper

8 slices multigrain bread

9 oz (250 g) smoked salmon, thinly sliced and cut into strips

1 organic lime, thinly sliced and cut into wedges

10 pitted black olives, sliced

Wash the lettuce, separating the leaves, and leave some water on the leaves.
Heat the olive oil in a saucepan with the garlic.
Add the lettuce leaves and season with salt and pepper.
Cook for a few minutes, then remove the garlic and puree the lettuce in a food processor.
Cut the bread into small squares.
Spread with the lettuce puree and top with a curl of smoked salmon.
Add a lime wedge and a slice of black olive and serve.

For a stronger flavor, stir some grated lime zest into the lettuce puree.

Preparation time **15 minutes**
Cooking time **5 minutes**
Level **easy**

rustic goat's cheese and pancetta canapés

Ingredients for 4 servings

Canapés:

5½ oz (150 g) fresh, mild goat's milk cheese

salt and pepper

1 tbsp heavy cream

6 slices soft soy bread

1 tbsp extra-virgin olive oil

1 rosemary sprig

8 very thin slices pancetta or bacon

Beat the goat's cheese until creamy with the salt, pepper and cream. Spread onto the bread and cut into whatever shape is desired.
Alternatively cut the bread into small shapes, then top with quenelles of the cheese mixture.
Heat a wide non-stick frying pan with a drizzle of olive oil and the rosemary sprig.
Lay the pancetta or bacon in the pan and let brown well. Remove from the pan and pat dry with paper towels as soon as it becomes crisp.
Break it into pieces.
Top each canapé with a piece and serve immediately.

Quenelle is a French term referring to an oval shape, formed between the hands or using two tablespoons.

Preparation time **15 minutes**
Cooking time **3 minutes**
Level **easy**

smoked salmon and culatello canapés

Ingredients for 4 servings

Canapés:

12 chives, minced

7 tbsps (3½ oz or 100 g) butter, softened

8 slices soft sandwich bread

5½ oz (150 g) smoked salmon, thinly sliced and cut into strips

5½ oz (150 g) culatello di Zibello, thinly sliced and cut into strips

Garnish:

chives or salad leaves

pepper

Stir the minced chives into the butter. Cut the bread into small decorative shapes. Spread with the chive butter. Top each piece of bread with a curl of salmon and a curl of culatello.

Garnish with chives or salad leaves and serve with a sprinkling of pepper.

Culatello is a cured meat similar to prosciutto, made from the most highly prized part of the pig's thigh. It is cured for about a year in very damp cellars in the area around Parma.

Preparation time **10 minutes**
Level **easy**

squash spread

Ingredients for 4 servings

Squash:

3 tbsps extra-virgin olive oil

1/2 yellow onion, minced

1/2 round, green-skinned winter squash, deseeded, peeled and diced

1/4 Savoy cabbage, thinly sliced

salt and pepper

thyme

2 cups (500 ml) hot vegetable broth

2 drops essential nutmeg oil

4 slices whole-wheat or kamut bread

Heat the olive oil and sauté the onion until soft. Add the squash and sauté for 3 minutes.
Add the Savoy cabbage, salt and pepper and cook for 3-4 minutes.
Add the thyme and a little hot broth and cook for another 15-20 minutes, covered, adding more broth as necessary.
Remove from the heat, let cool and add the nutmeg oil.
Puree in a food processor or blender until smooth.
Cut the bread into strips.
Serve the squash puree with the bread strips.

The Romans, gourmands that they were, used to eat raw Savoy cabbage before banquets to help their stomachs absorb the alcohol better. They also believed the vegetable had the ability to cure melancholy.

Preparation time **10 minutes**
Cooking time **30 minutes**
Level **easy**

canapés with mandarin butter and caviar

Ingredients for 4 servings

Canapés:

3/4 cup (6½ oz or 180 g) butter

grated zest of **1** organic mandarin

10½ oz (300 g) fresh white sandwich bread

freshly ground white pepper

3 tbsps caviar

Work the butter with a spatula until creamy and soft. Stir in the grated mandarin zest.
Spread the butter on a piece of wax paper and roll up into a cylinder. Refrigerate until firm.
Cut the bread into slices and remove the crusts.
Remove the butter from the refrigerator and work it again with a spatula until soft.
Spread the bread slices with the butter and sprinkle over a little white pepper.
Cut the bread into shapes (triangles, circles or squares, as desired) and top with a little caviar.
Optionally, garnish with small pieces of mandarin zest.

The mandarin originated in China and was introduced to Europe more than a century ago. It spread quickly, thanks to its delicate flavor. The rind is rich in an aromatic essential oil used to make liqueurs and sweets.

Preparation time **10 minutes**
Level **easy**

eggplant and robiola canapés

Ingredients for 4 servings
Canapés:

8 oz (220 g) robiola cheese

1 tsp dried oregano

salt and pepper

6-8 slices sandwich bread

10 slices grilled eggplant in oil

Beat the robiola with the oregano, salt and pepper until smooth and creamy.
Cut off the bread crusts, and spread the slices with the robiola cream.
Drain the eggplant from the oil and lay on top of the slices, overlapping slightly so as to completely cover the bread.
Cut into squares and serve.

Instead of using jarred eggplant, prepare it at home: Thinly slice a large eggplant and place in a colander. Salt the slices and place a weight on top. Leave to drain for 30 minutes. Rinse them, dry them and then cook on a hot ridged grill pan for 3 minutes on each side. Let marinate in extra-virgin olive oil with a little salt, garlic and a whole dried chili pepper.

Preparation time **10 minutes**
Level **easy**

truffled canapés

Ingredients for 4 servings

Canapés:

2 eggs

salt and pepper

1 tbsp extra-virgin olive oil

3 tbsps truffle butter

8 thin slices whole-wheat bread

Beat the eggs with a little salt and pepper.
Heat a wide non-stick frying pan with the olive oil.
Pour in the eggs and spread out to make a thin omelet.
Flip over and cook for 1 more minute, then let cool.
Cut the cooled omelet into thin strips.
Spread the truffle butter on the bread and top with the omelet strips.
Cut into triangles or other shapes and serve.

198

For more truffle flavor, top the canapés with some thin shavings of black truffle, either fresh or preserved.

Preparation time **20 minutes**
Cooking time **5 minutes**
Level **easy**

roasted pepper tartines

Ingredients for 4 servings
Tartines:

2 medium yellow-fleshed potatoes

salt and pepper

1 small red bell pepper

3 tbsps extra-virgin olive oil

2 tbsps fresh, spreadable cheese

5 slices white sandwich bread

5 slices whole-wheat sandwich bread

Place the potatoes in a pan with cold salted water and bring to a boil. Cook until just tender in the center, then drain and peel.
Meanwhile halve the pepper and remove the seeds and white pith. Either grill for 7-8 minutes on a hot, ridged cast-iron grill pan, or roast for 15 minutes in a hot oven (400°F, 200°C or Gas Mark 6).
Close in a plastic bag and let steam.
When cooled, peel the pepper halves.
Place the pepper halves in a food processor with the potatoes, olive oil, salt and pepper and puree.
Let cool, then stir in the cream.
Mix well until smooth, then spread on the white bread.
Cover with whole-wheat bread, and cut out circles.

Canapés

The roasted pepper puree can be replaced by green olive tapenade or an artichoke pâté, mixed with a fresh goat's cheese or ricotta, olive oil and black pepper.

Preparation time **15 minutes**
Cooking time **30 minutes**
Level **easy**

salmon and goat's cheese mousse tartines

Ingredients for 4 servings

Tartines:

7 oz (200 g) smoked salmon, chopped

3 tbsps (1½ oz or 40 g) butter, chopped

5½ oz (160 g) fresh goat's milk cheese

3 tbsps extra-virgin olive oil

zest of 1 organic lemon

milk (optional)

1 bunch chives, minced

salt and white pepper

1 loaf sliced white sandwich bread, crusts removed

Place the smoked salmon, butter, goat's cheese, olive oil and lemon zest in a food processor.
Puree to a smooth cream. If the mixture is too thick, add a little milk. Stir in the chives, salt and white pepper with a wooden spoon, and beat with the spoon until soft.
Spread the mousse on half the slices of bread and top with the other half, pressing down with the hands.
Cut into triangles.
If not serving immediately, wrap in plastic wrap and store in the refrigerator.

The tartines can be enriched with the addition of pickled onions, gherkins or pickled mushrooms, reducing the quantity of salmon.

Preparation time **10 minutes**
Level **easy**

bruschette

Finger Foods

brioche with cumin butter and smoked salmon

Ingredients for 4 servings

Brioche:

8 thick slices brioche bread

1/2 cup (4 oz or 120 g) butter, softened

1/2 tsp ground cumin

9 oz (250 g) Scottish smoked salmon, thinly sliced and cut into strips

dill, minced

Garnish:

1 lemon

Cut the brioche into whatever shapes are desired (triangles, squares or circles) and toast briefly in a hot oven until crisp. Let cool.

Beat the softened butter with the cumin, then spread on the cooled toasts.

Top each one with a curl of smoked salmon and sprinkle with dill.

Garnish the serving plate with lemon rind or slices.

Butter is a very common ingredient in the kitchen, thanks to its versatility and flavor. It should be kept wrapped up and refrigerated, to prevent it becoming rancid or absorbing the flavors of other foods. Butter pairs very well with salmon.

Preparation time **10 minutes**
Cooking time **5 minutes**
Level **easy**

bruschetta with eggplant pâté

Ingredients for 4 servings
Bruschetta:

4 tbsps extra-virgin olive oil

1 shallot, minced

2 violet eggplants, diced

2 thyme sprigs, leaves only,
plus extra for garnish

7 oz (200 g) robiola cheese

salt and pepper

8 slices of bread

Heat 2 tablespoons olive oil in a non-stick frying pan and sauté the shallot. Add the eggplant and thyme and cook for 10-12 minutes.

As soon as the eggplant is tender, puree in a food processor with the robiola and adjust salt and pepper. Let cool.

Cut the bread into shapes and brush with oil.

Toast under the broiler until crisp on both sides.

Form the cooled mixture into quenelles and serve on the hot toasts.

Garnish with a few thyme leaves.

Bruschette

The robiola can be replaced by another fresh cheese, like a mild goat's milk cheese or ricotta. If using a bitter eggplant, remove the seeds before cooking.

Preparation time **20 minutes**
Cooking time **15 minutes**
Level **easy**

radicchio and ricotta crostini

Ingredients for 4 servings
Crostini:
1/2 baguette
2 tbsps extra-virgin olive oil
2 shallots, minced
1/2 radicchio, finely chopped
1 tbsp balsamic vinegar
salt
5½ oz (150 g) fresh ricotta
chives, minced, plus whole for garnish
1 tsp grated ginger

Slice the baguette and toast in a hot oven for a few minutes.
Heat the olive oil and sauté the shallot until soft.
Add the radicchio, balsamic vinegar and a pinch of salt and cook over low heat for 5 minutes.
Beat the ricotta with a fork until creamy.
Stir in the minced chives and ginger.
Spread the toasts with the ricotta mixture and top with a quenelle of radicchio.
Garnish with chives.

The ricotta can be replaced with Gorgonzola, beaten until creamy with a little mascarpone, or with robiola.

Preparation time **15 minutes**
Cooking time **10 minutes**
Level **easy**

kamut crostini with winter vegetables

Ingredients for 4 servings
Crostini:

10½ oz (300 g) kamut bread

5-6 cauliflower florets

3 tbsps sesame oil, **1** garlic clove

2 cups (5½ oz or 150 g) sliced mushrooms

1 leek, julienned

1 celery stalk, diced, **1** carrot, diced

soy sauce, salt

3 tbsps tahini

Slice the bread and cut it into squares. Toast under the broiler for a few minutes, turning so it browns evenly on both sides.
Blanch the cauliflower florets in boiling water until tender. Drain and roughly chop.
Heat 1 tablespoon sesame oil in a frying pan with the garlic and sauté the mushrooms.
In another frying pan heat another tablespoon of sesame oil and sauté the leeks.
Add the celery and carrot and let cook for 10 minutes.
Stir in the soy sauce.
Mix all the vegetables together in a bowl and salt to taste.
Thin the tahini with a little olive oil and stir into the vegetables.
Top each toast with the vegetable mixture and serve hot.

Kamut is an ancient grain, an ancestor of modern wheat. It was first cultivated in ancient times in an area between Egypt and Mesopotamia, and after centuries of oblivion it has recently been rediscovered and again appreciated for its unique qualities.

Preparation time **15 minutes**
Cooking time **15 minutes**
Level **easy**

nut bread with apples and foie gras

Ingredients for 4 servings

Bread:

1 tsp active dry yeast

1/2 cup (125 ml) warm water

3 tbsps (1½ oz or 40 g) butter, salt

2 cups (9 oz or 250 g) all-purpose flour

2 cups (7 oz or 200 g) mixed nuts
(pine nuts, walnuts, pistachios,
cashews, hazelnuts), roughly chopped

Topping:

1 tab of butter

1 yellow apple, peeled and diced

1 tbsp passito dessert wine, pepper

7 oz (200 g) foie gras au torchon, sliced

Dissolve the yeast in the warm water and stir in the butter and salt.
Mix the flour and nuts together in a bowl.
Pour in the yeast mixture and mix together to form a dough. Form into a rope and let rise in a warm place.
Preheat the oven to 375°F (190°C or Gas Mark 5).
Bake the loaf for about 50 minutes and let cool.
Melt the butter for the topping in a non-stick frying pan.
Sauté the diced apple, deglazing the pan with the passito wine. Continue cooking until the liquid evaporates.
Season with pepper.
Slice the nut bread and top with the sautéed apples and a slice of foie gras.

If buying nuts in bulk, it is better
to choose ones still in their shells,
mainly for hygienic reasons.

Preparation time **30 minutes**
Cooking time **55 minutes**
Level **easy**

tuscan chicken liver crostini

Ingredients for 4 servings
Crostini:

10½ oz (300 g) chicken livers

5 tbsps white wine vinegar

1/2 baguette, sliced

4 tbsps extra-virgin olive oil

1 yellow onion, minced

sage, minced

1/4 cup (60 ml) red wine

1¼ cups (300 ml) hot vegetable broth

salt and pepper

10-15 salted capers, rinsed

5 anchovy fillets in oil, drained

Wash the chicken livers and place in a bowl with the vinegar and a little water.
Let marinate for 10 minutes, then rinse and set aside.
Toast the baguette slices under a broiler for a few minutes on each side.
Heat the olive oil and sauté the onion with the sage.
Add the chicken livers and brown briefly.
Add the wine, let cook for 2-3 minutes, then add the hot broth, salt and pepper.
Continue cooking until the liquid has evaporated.
Puree the mixture in a food processor together with the capers and anchovies.
Let the mixture sit for 20 minutes. If too thick, stir in a little hot broth.
Serve the chicken liver puree on the toasted bread.

Chicken livers should be carefully cleaned, and care should be taken to remove any veins, which can give the final dish a bitter taste.

Preparation time **25 minutes**
Cooking time **10 minutes**
Level **easy**

crostini with pea puree and prosciutto

Ingredients for 4 servings

Crostini:

2 tbsps extra-virgin olive oil

1 shallot, minced

1½ cups (200 g) spring peas

3/4 cup plus 1 tbsp (200 ml) vegetable broth

salt and pepper

8 slices sandwich bread

1½ oz (40 g) mild pecorino cheese, shaved

2½ oz (70 g) prosciutto, thinly sliced and cut into strips

Heat the olive oil in a small saucepan and sauté the shallot. As soon as it is transparent and soft, add the peas and the vegetable broth. Season with salt and pepper and cook for 12 minutes.

Meanwhile cut the bread into circles and toast under the broiler or on a hot grill.

Puree the peas in a food processor to obtain a thick cream. Let cool.

Spread the toasts with the cooled pea puree.

Top with a shaving of pecorino and a curl of prosciutto. Serve immediately.

The classic Italian combination of peas and prosciutto or pancetta is documented in one of the earliest cookbooks, that by Maestro Martino from around 1450.

Preparation time **10 minutes**
Cooking time **12 minutes**
Level **easy**

caramelized onion and foie gras crostoni on mortadella puree

Ingredients for 4 servings
Crostoni:
2 tbsps extra-virgin olive oil
2 sweet red onions, thinly sliced into rings
1 tsp peppercorns
1/2 cup (120 ml) Vin Santo wine, salt
4 slices Altamura-style bread
7 oz (200 g) foie gras, sliced
5 tbsps shelled pistachios, minced
Puree:
2 tbsps extra-virgin olive oil
1 garlic clove, **1** bay leaf
1 cup (4 oz or 120 g) minced celery, carrot and onion
5½ oz (150 g) mortadella, diced
1¾ cups (400 ml) vegetable broth
salt and pepper

The sweetest Italian onions are the flat red onions of Tropea, grown in an area with a very stable and mild microclimate during the winter.

Heat the olive oil for the puree in a saucepan with the garlic clove and bay leaf. Sauté the celery, carrot and onion, then add the mortadella and sauté for 4 minutes. Add the broth and cook over low heat for 15 minutes. Remove the garlic and bay and puree the mixture in a food processor or blender. Adjust salt and pepper.
Heat the olive oil for the crostoni and sauté the onions with the peppercorns.
Add the Vin Santo and salt and continue cooking over low heat, adding a little hot water when necessary, until the onions are soft. Toast the bread.
Heat a non-stick frying pan and sear the foie gras slices, then slice again.
Compose plates with the mortadella puree topped with a piece of toast, topped with onions and pieces of foie gras. Sprinkle with pistachios and serve.

Preparation time **20 minutes**
Cooking time **40 minutes**
Level **medium**

flavorful mediterranean focaccia

Ingredients for 4 servings

Focaccia:

7 oz (200 g) sheep's milk ricotta

5-6 basil leaves, minced

salt and pepper

9 oz (250 g) Ligurian focaccia

8 pitted black olives

7 large capers in brine, drained, rinsed and squeezed out

4 anchovy fillets, drained

Preheat the oven to 350°F (180°C or Gas Mark 4).
Beat the ricotta until creamy with the basil,
salt and pepper.
Cut the focaccia into small wedges, 1½ inches (4 cm) long,
and toast in the oven for 3-4 minutes. Let cool.
Mince the olives, capers and anchovies together with
a knife.
Spread a little of the ricotta mixture on one side of each
piece of focaccia.
Top with a little of the olive mixture and serve immediately.

Capers can be preserved in salt, vinegar or brine. They are most commonly used in southern Italy, where they can be found in all kinds of dishes, sauces and dressings.

Preparation time **10 minutes**
Cooking time **5 minutes**
Level **easy**

salt cod and leek crostini

Ingredients for 6 servings
Cod:

3 tbsps extra-virgin olive oil

2 leeks, sliced into thin rings

3 cups (700 ml) hot water

1 pinch of saffron

pepper

1 lb (500 g) salt cod, soaked, desalted and chopped

bread, sliced

1 bunch of parsley, minced

Heat the olive oil in a frying pan and add the leeks. Sauté for about 8 minutes, until almost transparent. Add the hot water, saffron and pepper.
As soon as the water comes to a boil, add the salt cod. Cook for 20 minutes.
Toast the bread slices, then serve the salt cod mixture on top of the toast, sprinkled with minced parsley.

For a variation, add minced black olives and pine nuts to the salt cod mixture.

Preparation time **15 minutes**
Cooking time **30 minutes**
Level **easy**

foie gras crostini with onion jam

Ingredients for 4 servings

Jam:

2 red onions, thinly sliced into rings

1 tbsp extra-virgin olive oil

1/2 cup (120 ml) full-bodied red wine

3 tbsps sugar

Crostini:

1/2 soft baguette

12½ oz (350 g) cleaned foie gras, cold

salt and pepper

Garnish:

chives (optional)

Wash the onion rings in a bowl of cold water and drain.
Heat the olive oil in a saucepan and sauté the onions.
Let cook over low heat for 20 minutes then add the wine.
Sprinkle over the sugar and continue cooking until
the onions are completely soft and caramelized.
As soon as all the liquid has evaporated, remove from
the heat and let cool.
Slice the bread along the diagonal and toast in the oven
or in a toaster.
Make sure the foie gras is very cold, and slice it with
a very sharp knife, cutting slices the same size as the
bread slices.
Heat a non-stick frying pan and sear the foie gras slices
until browned on the surface. Season with salt and pepper.
Serve the foie gras on top of the toasted bread,
accompanied by a little onion jam.
Garnish with chives, if desired.

Foie gras is a very refined food, not to
be recommended as part of a low-fat
diet, but delicious none the less.
The French have a saying about their
delicacy: "It stays on the tongue for
five seconds, in the stomach for five
hours and on the hips for five years."

Preparation time **30 minutes**
Cooking time **35 minutes**
Level **easy**

mushroom and roasted pepper toasts

Ingredients for 4 servings

Roasted:

1 red bell pepper, halved

3 large mushrooms, peeled and finely chopped

juice of **1/2** lemon

2 tbsps extra-virgin olive oil

salt and pepper

parsley, minced

8 slices sandwich bread

Remove the seeds and pith from the bell pepper and cook under the broiler until blackened. Close in a plastic bag to steam.
Meanwhile toss the chopped mushrooms with lemon juice, olive oil and salt.
Peel the bell pepper and finely chop the flesh.
Mix together the mushrooms, bell pepper and parsley.
Season to taste with pepper.
Cut the bread into disks using a round cookie cutter.
Toast in the oven until golden-brown.
Top the toasts with the mushroom mixture and serve.

Cookie cutters can be many shapes. Round cutters with high edges can be very useful in the kitchen, not just for cutting out circles of dough or bread, but also for shaping food while plating to create attractive presentations.

Preparation time **15 minutes**
Cooking time **10 minutes**
Level **easy**

avocado and speck crostini

Ingredients for 4 servings
Crostini:
1 ripe but firm avocado
salt and pepper
2 tbsps extra-virgin olive oil
1 piece fresh ginger, grated
4 slices sandwich bread
6 slices smoked speck, julienned

Peel the avocado. Halve lengthwise, remove the pit and dice the flesh. Place in a bowl and mix with salt, pepper, olive oil and a little of the grated ginger.
Cut out 4 circles of 2 inches (5 cm) in diameter from the bread with a round cookie cutter, and toast them under the broiler or in a non-stick frying pan, sprinkling them with a little salt.
Place the bread circles on plates while still warm.
Use the cookie cutter to shape the avocado on top of the bread, leveling off the top with the back of a teaspoon.
Top the avocado with julienned speck.
Place the rest of the ginger in a bowl with the olive oil and let sit for 5 minutes.
Whisk with a fork and then strain through a small sieve.
Drizzle the crostini with ginger oil and serve.

Avocado, also known as avocado pear because of its shape, is native to Mexico. It is cultivated in tropical and Mediterranean climates, is very high in calories, and is more often used as a vegetable than a fruit.

Preparation time **20 minutes**
Cooking time **4 minutes**
Level **easy**

crostini with parsley mushrooms

Ingredients for 4 servings

Crostini:

8 mushrooms

juice of **1/2** lemon

3 tbsps extra-virgin olive oil

salt and pepper

1 bunch parsley, minced

5 chives, minced, plus extra whole for garnish

1 garlic clove, green shoot removed, minced

1 baguette

Carefully peel the mushrooms, starting from the base of the cap. Take hold of the skin and carefully pull up until reaching the top. Repeat until fully peeled.
Cut off the earthy part of the stem. Carefully wash the mushrooms.
Using a sharp knife, roughly chop the mushrooms. Place in a bowl and immediately dress with lemon juice (to stop discoloration), oil, salt and abundant pepper.
Stir the parsley, chives and garlic into the mushroom mixture and refrigerate for 30 minutes.
Slice the baguette and toast for a few minutes under the broiler.
Serve the mushrooms on top of the toast, garnished with chives.

Garlic is indispensable to the cuisines of many countries. It is also valued for its medicinal properties. One cure for the common cold involves holding a whole garlic clove in the mouth, between the teeth and the inner cheek, for two hours. Try it and see!

232

Preparation time **20 minutes**
Level **easy**

mussel and tomato bruschetta

Ingredients for 4 servings
Bruschetta:
10½ oz (300 g) mussels
2 tbsps extra-virgin olive oil
1 garlic clove
1/2 dried red chili pepper
2 tomatoes
parsley, minced
salt and pepper
6 slices crusty bread

Wash and debeard the mussels. Heat the olive oil, garlic and chile in a frying pan and add the mussels. Cover and cook over high heat for 5 minutes, until the mussels open. Blanch the tomatoes, drain and cool in ice water. Peel, deseed and chop the flesh.
Shell the mussels and strain their cooking liquid.
Place the mussels and liquid in a small saucepan with the parsley and cook down until the liquid is reduced. Stir in the tomatoes, salt and pepper and keep warm.
Cut the bread into pieces, toast and top with the mussels and tomatoes.

Mussels should be cleaned under running water, pulling away the beard and brushing them with a metal brush or steel wool.

Preparation time **15 minutes**
Cooking time **10 minutes**
Level **easy**

pecorino and mostarda crostini

Ingredients for 4 servings

Crostini:

4 slices country-style bread, cut into **1/3**-inch (1 cm) strips

9 oz (250 g) semi-aged mild pecorino, cut into 1/3-inch (1 cm) strips

2 tbsps fruit mostarda, finely chopped

Preheat the broiler. Lay the bread strips on a baking sheet and top each one with a strip of pecorino.
Broil until the cheese is melted, then sprinkle over the mostarda.
Serve immediately.

Mostarda is preserved fruit in a spicy, mustard-spiked syrup. It could be replaced with a red onion jam or sweet wine jelly, perhaps with a goat's cheese instead of pecorino. A selection of different crostini could be served together.

Preparation time **10 minutes**
Cooking time **4 minutes**
Level **easy**

thyme and eggplant crostini

Ingredients for 4 servings
Crostini:

1 large or 2 medium eggplants, cubed

salt and pepper

3 tbsps extra-virgin olive oil

1 onion, minced

2 thyme sprigs, leaves only.

4 slices sandwich bread, cut into strips

Garnish:

chives (optional)

fried strips of eggplant skin (optional)

Place the eggplant cubes in a colander and sprinkle with salt. Place a weight on top (for example a plate and a bowl of water) and let drain for 30 minutes.

Heat the olive oil and sauté the onion over low heat until soft. Add the eggplant and cook gently, covered, stirring every so often. At first it might seem to dry, but the eggplant will gradually release its liquid.

Add the thyme and a pinch of pepper and let cook for about 15 minutes.

Transfer the mixture to a food processor and puree until smooth. Let cool completely.

Toast the bread strips and serve, spread with the eggplant puree. Garnish with chives or fried strips of eggplant skin, as desired.

This same puree can be used as a pasta sauce or to fill crêpes. With the addition of 2 egg yolks and 2 tablespoons of grated Parmesan cheese, it can make an excellent filling for stuffed vegetables.

Preparation time **20 minutes**
Cooking time **15 minutes**
Level **medium**

whole-wheat toasts
with caponata and mozzarella

Ingredients for 4 servings

Toasts:

1/2 onion, minced

2 tbsps extra-virgin olive oil

1 wedge pumpkin or Kabocha squash, peeled, deseeded and chopped

1 celery stalk, diced

1/2 eggplant, diced

1 garlic clove, smashed

salt and pepper

5 cherry tomatoes, sliced

2 small potatoes, boiled, peeled and sliced

1/2 whole-wheat baguette

5½ oz (150 g) cow's milk mozzarella, sliced

Preheat the oven to 400°F (200°C or Gas Mark 6).
Sauté the onion in the olive oil in a large frying pan.
When brown, add the pumpkin and celery, cook for a few minutes, then add the eggplant.
Add the garlic, salt and pepper to taste and a few tablespoons of water. Let simmer until the vegetables are soft, then add the tomatoes, potatoes and salt and pepper to taste. Set aside.
Slice the baguette and place on a baking sheet.
Cover each slice of bread with a thin slice of mozzarella and a generous spoonful of the vegetable mixture.
Bake for three minutes or until the mozzarella begins to melt. Serve hot.

Browning refers to sautéing an ingredient until it becomes golden-brown and its flavors intensify. It is usually used for onions and meat.

Preparation time **15 minutes**
Cooking time **30 minutes**
Level **easy**

roast pork sandwiches
with spring onion salsa

Ingredients for 4 servings

Sandwiches:

1 handful baby spinach leaves

8 slices sandwich bread

7 oz (200 g) roast pork or veal,
thinly sliced

Salsa:

2 bunches spring onions, trimmed

10 sage leaves

4 tbsps extra-virgin olive oil

2 tbsps white wine

2 tsps hot mustard

salt and pepper

Place the spring onions in a food processor with the sage, olive oil, wine and mustard, and chop finely.
Season to taste with salt and pepper.
Rinse the baby spinach under cold running water and pat dry.
Cover half the bread slices with a layer of spinach leaves. Top with a slice of pork or veal and then spread over the spring onion salsa.
Cover with the remaining slice of bread and cut the sandwiches in half diagonally.

As it uses raw spring onions, the salsa will have a strong pungency which might not be to everyone's taste. For a milder flavor, blanch the spring onions for 1-2 minutes in boiling salted water before proceeding with the recipe.

Preparation time **15 minutes**
Level **easy**

robiola and prosciutto crostini

Ingredients for 4 servings
Crostini:
4 slices soft sandwich bread
3 oz (80 g) robiola cheese
2 tbsps finely chopped walnuts
chives, minced
salt and pepper
2 oz (60 g) prosciutto, sliced
Garnish:
chives
1/4 avocado, diced

Cut the bread into triangles and toast it under the broiler.
Beat the robiola into a cream with the walnuts, chives, salt and pepper, using a wooden spoon.
Reserve 1 slice of prosciutto for garnish, and finely chop the rest. Stir into the robiola mixture.
Cut the reserved slice of prosciutto into thin strips.
Place a spoonful of the robiola mixture on each toast and garnish with prosciutto strips, chives and diced avocado.

244

Robiola is a fresh, unaged cheese, shaped in a cylinder and made all year round from the milk of cows, goats and sheep.

Preparation time **15 minutes**
Cooking time **3 minutes**
Level **easy**

seitan crostini with cannellini puree

Ingredients for 4 servings

Crostini:

1 cup (7 oz or 200 g) dried cannellini beans

1 piece of kombu seaweed

1 tbsp salted capers, rinsed

1/2 spring onion, chopped, **1/2** lemon

2 tbsps extra-virgin olive oil

1 tbsp corn oil

12½ oz (350 g) kamut seitan, sliced

Garnish:

1/2 lemon, thinly sliced, **1** tbsp capers

1/2 spring onion, minced

Seitan is made from wheat gluten, and has a firm, meaty texture. It is usually sold in square or rectangular bricks. It is best to prepare it with beans, which enhance and complement its nutritional qualities.

Soak the beans in cold water overnight. Cook them in a pressure cooker with the piece of seaweed for 1 hour. Drain the cooked beans and place them in a food processor with the capers, spring onion, a squeeze of lemon juice and olive oil. Puree to a smooth cream. Heat the corn oil in a non-stick frying pan and brown the seitan slices.

Spread the bean puree on the slices of warm seitan and garnish with lemon slices, capers and minced spring onion.

Preparation time **20 minutes**
Cooking time **1 hour 15 minutes**
Level **easy**

lardo and tomato crostini

Ingredients for 4 servings
Crostini:

1 tbsp extra-virgin olive oil

4 thick slices country-style bread, baked in wood-fired oven

1 San Marzano or plum tomato

salt and pepper

5½ oz (150 g) Colonnata lardo (cured lard), thinly sliced

rosemary leaves

Preheat the oven to 425°F (220°C or Gas Mark 7). Oil the surface of the bread and cut the slices into quarters. Toast in the oven until golden.
Blanch the tomato for one minute, then immerse in iced water. Peel, deseed and dice.
Season with salt and pepper.
Place 1 slice of lardo on each toast then top with some tomato and a rosemary leaf.
Sprinkle with pepper and serve.

Lardo from Colonnata in Tuscany is made by placing pieces of lard in a container made from a block of marble, called a conca. The lard is laid on top of a bed of coarse sea salt, ground black pepper, peeled fresh garlic, rosemary and sage. The conca is closed with a marble lid and the lard cures for at least six months.

Preparation time **10 minutes**
Cooking time **10 minutes**
Level **easy**

porcini mushroom crostini

Ingredients for 4 servings

Crostini:

3 large fresh porcini mushrooms
(about 10½ oz or 300 g)

2 tbsps extra-virgin olive oil

1 tab of butter

2 garlic cloves, smashed

parsley, minced

thyme leaves

salt and pepper

4 thick slices of crusty bread, toasted

Carefully clean the porcini using a paper towel,
then chop them.
Heat the olive oil and butter in a non-stick frying pan
with the garlic. When it starts to color, add
the mushrooms and brown them.
Mix together the parsley, thyme, salt and pepper
and add to the mushrooms.
Serve the mushroom mixture on top of the toasted bread.

Though better known outside of Italy
in their dried form, fresh porcini
are also a delicacy. Available in the
autumn, they grow wild in forests.
They can also be known as king
bolete, cep or penny bun.

Preparation time **10 minutes**
Cooking time **15 minutes**
Level **easy**

eggplant crostini with crispy peppers

Ingredients for 4 servings

Crostini:

1 medium yellow-fleshed potato

2 tbsps extra-virgin olive oil

1 shallot, minced

1 large eggplant, diced

salt and pepper, thyme

1 baguette, sunflower oil

1/2 red bell pepper, julienned

1/2 yellow bell pepper, julienned

2 tbsps finely ground cornmeal

Preheat the oven to 350°F (180°C or Gas Mark 4).
Boil the potato until just cooked through,
then drain and peel.
Heat the olive oil and sauté the shallot over low heat.
As soon as it is translucent, add the eggplant and a little
salt and pepper. Cover and continue cooking, stirring
frequently with a wooden spoon to avoiding sticking and
to make sure the eggplant cooks evenly. As soon as
the eggplant softens, stir in the thyme and let cool.
Place the eggplant and potato in a food processor
and puree until smooth.
Slice the baguette and toast the slices in the oven
for 5 minutes.
Heat the sunflower oil. Dip the pepper strips in
the cornmeal and then fry them until crispy.
Drain on paper towels.
Spread the eggplant puree on the toasts and top with
a few strips of pepper.

There are differences in opinion regarding which parts of the eggplant to use and which to discard. Some advocate removing the central, seedy part, some peel the eggplant, and others use everything, especially if the eggplants are small.

Preparation time **15 minutes**
Cooking time **30 minutes**
Level **easy**

baguette toasts with artichoke pâté and speck

Ingredients for 4 servings

Baguette:

1/2 baguette

1 tbsp extra-virgin olive oil

5½ oz (150 g) artichoke pâté

4 oz (120 g) speck, thinly sliced, cut into strips

Slice the baguette and place on a baking sheet.
Oil the top of the bread with a little extra-virgin olive oil and toast under the broiler until golden.
Top the toasts with a little artichoke pâté and a curl of speck, made by rolling up a strip.

To make artichoke pâté at home, puree 5½ oz (150 g) baby artichokes in oil in a food processor.

Preparation time **15 minutes**
Cooking time **15 minutes**
Level **easy**

Bruschette

254

crostini with zucchini and shrimp

Ingredients for 4 servings

Crostini:

2 tbsps extra-virgin olive oil

1 garlic clove, smashed

2 large zucchini, green part only, diced

7 oz (200 g) shrimp, shelled and chopped

salt and pepper

2 tbsps hot vegetable broth or water

1/2 baguette

Heat a non-stick frying pan with the oil and garlic.
Add the zucchini and sauté over high heat for 2 minutes.
Add the shrimp and cook for another 2 minutes.
Season with salt and pepper.
Add the hot vegetable broth or water and keep warm.
Slice the bread into thin slices (about 1/5 inch or 1/2 cm) and toast under the broiler.
Top with the zucchini-shrimp mixture and serve hot.

Zucchini can be prepared in many different ways. Always wash and trim them before using. The flowers are also edible, and when purchasing look for ones which have just barely opened.

Preparation time **15 minutes**
Cooking time **8 minutes**
Level **easy**

crostini with capers and ricotta

Ingredients for 4 servings

Crostini:

7 tbsps (3½ oz or 100 g) butter, softened

1/2 tsp ground cumin

7 oz (200 g) fresh ricotta

1 gherkin, drained and rinsed

1 small onion, minced, chives, minced

1 tbsp capers, minced, plus extra for garnish

1/2 tsp mustard

salt and pepper, sliced rye bread

1/2 tsp sweet paprika

Beat the butter with an electric beater and mix in the cumin.
Sieve the ricotta and stir in the butter, gherkin, onion, chives, capers and mustard and season to taste with salt and pepper. Refrigerate.
Cut the bread into squares and toast under the broiler until golden.
Top with the ricotta mixture, either spreading it on or forming it into quenelles using two teaspoons.
Garnish with a pinch of paprika, and chives and capers if desired.

Bruschette

The best capers come from the Sicilian island of Pantelleria. They can be preserved in salt and stored in a jar for several years without losing their flavor.

Preparation time **15 minutes**
Cooking time **5 minutes**
Level **easy**

melted brie and porcini crostoni

Ingredients for 4 servings
Crostoni:

10 oz (280 g) brie cheese, thinly sliced

4 large slices country-style bread

4-5 medium-sized fresh porcini mushrooms

2 tbsps extra-virgin olive oil

salt and pepper

Lay the brie slices on the bread, leaving about
1/5 inch (1/2 cm) between each slice.
Carefully clean the mushrooms, cutting off the earthy part
of the stem and cleaning the cap with a damp paper towel.
Thinly slice and sauté in a frying pan with a drizzle of olive
oil for 1 minute.
Lay the mushrooms over the brie slices.
Season with salt and pepper and then broil until
the cheese has melted.
Serve immediately.

The crostoni could be finished
with a handful of finely
chopped arugula, which
would add a pleasant fresh
bitterness and bright color.

Preparation time **10 minutes**
Cooking time **5 minutes**
Level **easy**

baba ghannouj

Ingredients for 4 servings
Baba Ghannouj:
2 eggplants
6 slices sandwich bread
2 garlic cloves, smashed
3 tbsps tahini
juice of **1** lemon
salt
1 bunch parsley, minced
extra-virgin olive oil

Preheat the oven to 375°F (190°C or Gas Mark 5).
Prick the eggplants all over with a fork, then bake whole
in the oven for about 40 minutes, until soft.
Toast the bread under the broiler and cut into shapes
as desired.
Peel the cooked eggplants and place the flesh in a bowl.
Mash together with the garlic, tahini, lemon juice and salt.
Stir well, then cover with plastic wrap and leave in a cool
place to let the flavors blend.
When ready to serve, arrange the baba ghannouj
in the center of a plate, topped with minced parsley
and a drizzle of olive oil.
Accompany with the toasted bread.

262

This is the most popular starter
in the Middle East, effectively an
eggplant puree, but with many
possible variations in preparation. The
name literally means "the spoiledfather."

Preparation time **15 minutes**
Cooking time **40 minutes**
Level **easy**

radicchio, provola and ham bruschetta

Ingredients for 4 servings
Bruschetta:

1 Treviso radicchio

3 tbsps (1½ oz or 40 g) butter

1 garlic clove, unpeeled and smashed

salt and pepper

8 slices country-style bread
(such as Altamura)

1 tbsp extra-virgin olive oil

7 oz (200 g) mild smoked provola
cheese, sliced or diced

5½ oz (150 g) ham, sliced and
torn into pieces

Remove the two outer leaves of the radicchio and the hard base. Finely chop the rest and carefully wash it.
Melt the butter in a saucepan and add the garlic.
Add the radicchio, salt and pepper, lower the heat and cook until tender and creamy.
Toast the bread under the broiler and lightly oil it.
Top the toast with the radicchio, the provola and the ham.
Broil for a few minutes, until the cheese melts, and serve immediately.

For even more flavor the ham can be replaced by pancetta or speck.

Preparation time **10 minutes**
Cooking time **10 minutes**
Level **easy**

spiced spinach and feta pies

Ingredients for 6-8 servings

Crust:

2 cups (9 oz or 250 g) all-purpose flour

1 tsp active dry yeast

2/3 cup (160 ml) warm water

3 tbsps (1½ oz or 40 g) melted butter

Filling:

7 oz (200 g) spinach, chopped

1/2 tsp ground cumin

1 tsp sweet paprika, **1/2** tsp chile powder

2 garlic cloves, minced, **1** onion, minced

salt and pepper, **7** oz (200 g) feta cheese

extra-virgin olive oil (optional)

Preheat the oven to 375°F (190°C or Gas Mark 5).
Sift the flour and yeast together and mix with the warm water and melted butter to make a smooth, elastic dough. Wrap in plastic wrap and refrigerate.
Mix together the spinach, cumin, paprika, chile powder, garlic, onion, salt and pepper.
Crumble over the feta and mix well, adding a drizzle of extra-virgin olive oil if necessary.
Roll the dough out thinly and use it to line the base of 8 small, round molds. Fill with the spinach mixture and top with another layer of dough.
Press down around the edges with fingertips to seal.
Bake for 30-35 minutes and serve immediately.

Different kinds of paprika have different levels of spiciness, and so it's important to taste a tiny amount before using it in a recipe, to avoid a dish being either overly hot or too bland.

Preparation time **25 minutes**
Cooking time **35 minutes**
Level **easy**

crostini with porcini pâté

Ingredients for 6 servings

Crostini:

3 large, dark, fresh porcini mushrooms

1/2 cup plus 2½ tbsps (5½ oz or 150 g) cold butter, chopped

1 shallot, minced

salt and pepper

1 egg

2 tbsps pine nuts

1/2 black truffle, shaved

4 slices Tuscan- or Puglian-style bread

Clean the porcini with damp paper towels and cut off the earthy part of the stalk. Chop and set aside. Melt half the butter in a small saucepan and sauté the shallot. Add the porcini and cook for 10 minutes, seasoning with salt and pepper.
Meanwhile hard-boil the egg.
Toast the pine nuts in a small non-stick frying pan. Add to the mushrooms and adjust salt and pepper. Let cool, then puree in a food processor with the remaining cold butter, hard-boiled egg and truffle. Place in a ceramic bowl and chill in the top part of the refrigerator.
Remove the pâté from the refrigerator 20 minutes before serving.
Toasl the bread and serve hot, spread with the porcini pâté.

268

Before using, check the condition of the pine nuts, whether recently bought or not. They can turn rancid in just a few days, and using them could mean spoiling the whole dish.

Preparation time **20 minutes**
Cooking time **20 minutes**
Level **easy**

eggs benedict on rye bread

Ingredients for 4 servings

Eggs Benedict:

3/4 cup (6 oz or 175 g) butter

4 egg yolks

2 tbsps water

2 tbsps white wine vinegar

4 slices of rye bread

8 slices of ham

4 cups (1 litre) water

8 eggs

salt and pepper

Melt the butter over a double boiler. Place the egg yolks, water and 1 tablespoon vinegar in a blender or food processor, and gradually pour in the hot butter while mixing to emulsify, forming a thick sauce.
Toast the bread on both sides and lay 2 slices of ham on each one.
Bring the water to boil in a large pan, add the remaining tablespoon of vinegar, and as soon as it starts boiling, poach the eggs by breaking them one at time onto a plate and adding them to the water after swirling the water with a spoon so that the egg white wraps itself around the yolk. As soon as they are cooked, drain them and immerse in cold water, then drain again and pat dry.
Lay 2 eggs on each slice of bread, season the sauce with salt and pepper to taste, and pour over.
Serve immediately, accompanied by a green salad or julienned fennel if desired.

Toasting means a dry cooking of foods, usually bread. Rice can also be toasted, usually in a saucepan with oil and butter, prior to the addition of a cooking liquid. During toasting the rice is stirred frequently to keep it from sticking. Toasting helps the rice grains stay al dente during cooking.

Preparation time **10 minutes**
Cooking time **10 minutes**
Level **medium**

petits fours

Finger Foods

pine-nut wafers with steamed apricots

Ingredients for 4 servings
Apricots:

8 small apricots, halved and pitted
2 cinnamon sticks, **4** mint leaves

Wafers:

3½ tbsps pine nuts, **2** egg whites
3/4 cup (3½ oz or 100 g)
confectioners' sugar
7 tbsps (3½ oz or 100 g) butter,
melted and cooled
1/2 cup plus 1 tbsp (2½ oz or 70 g)
all-purpose flour

Garnish:

2 tbsps sweetened creamy yogurt
fresh mint leaves, cinnamon sticks

Preheat the oven to 400°F (200°C or Gas Mark 6).
Place the apricot halves in a thick zip-lock plastic bag
with the cinnamon and mint. Close and steam
for 15 minutes, then let cool.
Grind the pine nuts in a food processor.
Beat the egg whites and confectioners' sugar together
with a whisk until fluffy but not stiff. Whisk in the cooled
melted butter in a thin stream, then the flour and ground
pine nuts. Refrigerate the batter for 10 minutes.
Line a baking sheet with parchment paper and place
spoonfuls of batter on it, forming a total of 16 small
circles. Bake for 5 minutes. As soon as they are golden,
remove from the oven and place the disks over small
upside-down cylindrical molds, so that as they cool
and harden they form small bowls.
Once cooled, turn them right side up and fill each one
with an apricot half. Top with a drop of creamy yogurt and
garnish with mint leaves and pieces of cinnamon.

The apricot tree belongs to the same
family as roses. Originally cultivated in
China 3,000 years ago, it then spread west,
until it reached Armenia. The Romans, who
introduced it to Europe 2,000 years ago,
called it armeniacum, "Armenian apple."

Preparation time **15 minutes**
Cooking time **15 minutes**
Level **easy**

zabaglione-filled cannoncini

Ingredients for 8 servings
Cannoncini:
14 oz (400 g) puff pastry
2 tbsps sugar
Zabaglione:
5 egg yolks
2/3 cup (4½ oz or 130 g) sugar
1/2 cup (120 ml) Marsala wine
1 tsp cornstarch
salt

Preheat the oven to 400°F (200°C or Gas Mark 6).
Cut the puff pastry into strips 1/2 inch (1 cm) wide and roll them around cylindrical aluminum molds, slightly overlapping the edges. Arrange them on a baking sheet lined with waxed paper and sprinkle them with sugar. Bake for about 18 minutes, until puffed up and golden. Remove from the oven and let cool.
Meanwhile beat the egg yolks in a stainless-steel bowl over a double boiler with the sugar and Marsala.
Add the cornstarch and a pinch of salt and continue cooking until the mixture increases in volume.
Transfer to a container and refrigerate.
Unmold the cannoncini and fill with the zabaglione, using a pastry bag or a large syringe.

A pastry bag is a large cone of plastic or fabric, with a hole in the tip. It can be filled with creams or icings and used to pipe them in decorative ways.

Preparation time **30 minutes**
Cooking time **40 minutes**
Level **medium**

mini cherry clafoutis

Ingredients for 6 servings

Clafoutis:

3 eggs

1 egg yolk

3/4 cup (5 oz or 135 g) raw cane sugar

1/2 tsp vanilla extract

1 cup (250 ml) heavy cream

1 cup (250 ml) milk

1½ tbsps (3/4 oz or 20 g) butter, melted

30 ripe cherries

confectioners' sugar

Preheat the oven to 375°F (190°C or Gas Mark 5).
Beat the eggs, egg yolk and raw cane sugar until creamy, then add the vanilla, cream, milk and melted butter.
Let rest for 15 minutes.
Fill paper baking cups two-thirds full with the mixture, then place 1 cherry in each one.
Arrange on a baking sheet and bake for about 20 minutes.
Serve warm, sprinkled with confectioners' sugar.

The same recipe can be used for the classic clafoutis, using a single large cake tin and cooking for an extra 2 minutes. Alternatively, use strawberries instead of cherries.

Preparation time **25 minutes**
Cooking time **20 minutes**
Level **easy**

mini date strudels

Ingredients for 4 servings
Strudel:

7 oz (200 g) pitted dates, halved

2 sticks of natural licorice, cut into strips

1 Golden Delicious apple, peeled, cored and diced

2/3 cup (2 oz or 60 g) walnuts, minced

2 tbsps sugar, **2** tsps acacia honey

9 oz (250 g) phyllo dough

3½ tbsps (2 oz or 50 g) melted butter

Sauce:

2 egg yolks, **4** tbsps sugar

1 tsp cornstarch, **1** cup (250 ml) milk

zest of **1** organic orange

3 tbsps heavy cream

Phyllo dough is a kind of very thin pastry which cooks very quickly, and is usually either fried or baked. It is commonly used in the Middle East to make traditional sweets.

Place the dates in a sous-vide bag with the licorice strips and seal with a sous-vide machine. Leave for 3 days, then remove the dates and chop them. Discard the licorice.
Preheat the oven to 350°F (180°C or Gas Mark 4).
Toss the apple with the sugar and let sit for 10 minutes.
Stir in the walnuts, dates and honey.
Lay out the phyllo dough, 2 sheets at a time.
Brush with melted butter. Sprinkle over the apple mixture and roll up the dough. Cut some incisions on the top to allow steam to escape. Brush with more melted butter and bake for 15-20 minutes.
Beat the egg yolks and sugar for the sauce and add the cornstarch. Bring the milk to a boil with the orange zest and pour onto the egg yolks in a thin stream, beating constantly. Return the mixture to the heat and cook over low heat until slightly thickened. Let cool.
Whip the cream.
Fold the whipped cream into the cooled sauce.
Cut the strudel into individual portions, and serve with the cream sauce.

Preparation time **25 minutes**
Cooking time **20 minutes**
Level **medium**

apple fritters with vin santo sauce

Ingredients for 4 servings
Fritters:

2 eggs, **4** tbsps all-purpose flour

3 tbsps cold milk

3½ tbsps sugar, salt

3 Red Delicious apples

breadcrumbs, extra-virgin olive oil

Sauce:

1 egg, **1** tbsp confectioners' sugar

3/4 cup (180 ml) Vin Santo wine

Garnish:

apple slices (optional)

fresh mint leaves (optional)

The Red Delicious apple is considered the apple par excellence. It has brilliant coloring, an elongated form and five points on the bottom. It is the most cultivated apple in the world, and can be found on the market during the winter.

Beat the eggs for the fritters in a bowl. Add 2 tablespoons flour and stir until it forms a thick batter.
Stir in the cold milk, sugar and a pinch of salt.
Peel the apples and cut into small balls using a melon baller. Dip them in flour, then the batter, and then breadcrumbs.
Heat the olive oil to about 350°F (180°C) and fry the apple balls until golden. Drain and dry on paper towels.
Meanwhile break the egg into a small copper bowl and add the confectioners' sugar and Vin Santo.
Place over a double boiler. Heat gently while whisking until thickened and creamy.
Pour the sauce in the center of a plate and top with the apple fritters. Garnish with apple slices and fresh mint, as desired.

Preparation time **20 minutes**
Cooking time **15 minutes**
Level **easy**

tartlets with orange-flower cream

Ingredients for 4 servings

Tartlets:

9 oz (250 g) phyllo dough

3½ tbsps (2 oz or 50 g) butter

Cream:

1¾ cups (400 ml) milk

1 tsp orange-flavored black tea

2 egg yolks, **1** piece vanilla bean

1½ oz (45 g) orange flowers

2½ tbsps sugar, salt

1/2 cup (2 oz or 60 g) cornstarch

7 tbsps heavy cream

Garnish:

maraschino or amarena

cherries in syrup, orange flowers

Preheat the oven to 350°F (180°C or Gas Mark 4).

Lay out the dough and make a stack of 4 layers, brushing with melted butter between each layer.

Using a cookie cutter, cut out circles big enough to line small tartlet molds. Line the molds and prick the bottom with a fork. Bake for 10 minutes.

Bring the milk to a boil with the tea, vanilla bean and orange flowers. Remove from the heat, cover and let infuse for 10 minutes.

Beat the egg yolks with the sugar and a pinch of salt. Add the cornstarch. Strain the milk and add to the egg mixture. Return to the heat and cook over low heat, whisking constantly.

When thickened, remove from the heat and let cool. Whip the cream and fold into the sauce. Refrigerate.

Just before serving, fill the phyllo tartlets with the cream, garnishing with cherries and orange flowers.

Black tea, as well as being a source of antioxidants, also has antibacterial and protective properties for our teeth, being rich in polyphenols and fluoride.

Preparation time **30 minutes**
Cooking time **20 minutes**
Level **easy**

sweet mushrooms with two creams

Ingredients for 8 servings
Mushrooms:

4 egg yolks

2/3 cup (4 oz or 120 g) sugar

1/2 tsp vanilla extract, salt

2 cups (500 ml) milk

2½ oz (70 g) dark chocolate, chopped

20 puff-pastry mushrooms

unsweetened cocoa powder

Beat the egg yolks with the sugar, vanilla and a pinch of salt until creamy.
Heat the milk, and when it starts to boil pour it over the eggs, whisking constantly. Return the mixture to the heat and continue cooking, whisking constantly, until it thickens. Stir most of the chocolate into half the cream, stirring until melted. Chill the two creams.
Melt the remaining chocolate.
Fill the stalks of the mushrooms with the chocolate cream and the caps with the plain vanilla cream.
Stick the two halves together with melted chocolate.
Let cool. Sprinkle with cocoa powder and serve.

Cacao contains caffeine and theobromine, which together affect the cardiovascular and muscular systems and have a positive effect on mental concentration and physical energy.

Preparation time **20 minutes**
Cooking time **15 minutes**
Level **easy**

sicilian cannoli

Ingredients for 4 servings
Cannoli:
5½ oz (150 g) ricotta

6 tbsps confectioners' sugar

1 oz (25 g) candied orange and citron peel, minced

2½ tbsps (1 oz or 30 g) dark chocolate chips

1 tsp orange-flower water

10 ready-made cannoli

Garnish:
confectioners' sugar

Pass the ricotta through a sieve and beat it with the confectioners' sugar until creamy.
Stir in the candied citrus peel, chocolate drops and orange-flower water.
Fill the cannoli with the ricotta mixture.
Sprinkle with confectioners' sugar and serve.

Orange-flower water is made from the maceration and distillation of flowers from Seville oranges, so-called "bitter" oranges. A typical ingredient in Neapolitan pastries, it is often used in confectionery to flavor sweets and creams.

Preparation time **10 minutes**
Level **medium**

sweet apple and radicchio fritters

Ingredients for 4 servings
Fritters:

1 Golden Delicious apple

juice of **1/2** lemon

2 tbsps raw cane sugar

1 cinnamon stick, **1** clove

4 slices brioche bread
(about 4 oz or 120 g)

3 tbsps milk, **1** tbsp Marsala wine

1/2 Treviso radicchio, **2** eggs

3 tbsps sugar

3/4 cup (3½ oz or 100 g) breadcrumbs

sunflower oil

Peel and core the apple, reserving the peel.
Chop the flesh and sprinkle with lemon juice.
Place the apple peel in a small saucepan with the raw
cane sugar, cinnamon and clove.
Cover with water and cook for 15 minutes over low heat.
Soak the brioche in the milk and Marsala.
Remove the white stalks of the radicchio and slice
the rest into julienne strips.
Drain the brioche and squeeze out excess liquid.
Beat the eggs and the sugar and stir in the apple,
radicchio and brioche. Beat with a wooden spoon,
then form the mixture into small balls.
Chill them, then coat with breadcrumbs.
Discard the clove and cinnamon from the apple peel
infusion. Puree the infusion in a food processor,
then pass through a sieve.
Heat the sunflower oil and fry the apple fritters,
draining them on paper towels. Roll in a little sugar
and serve with the cold apple-peel sauce.

When buying radicchio, look for heads
which have a bright red color, with no
wilting or wrinkling on the leaves.

Preparation time **30 minutes**
Cooking time **25 minutes**
Level **easy**

soft millefeuille with lemon and pistachio

Ingredients for 8 servings

Millefeuille:

4 egg yolks

2/3 cup (4 oz or 125 g) sugar

grated zest of **2** organic lemons

6 tbsps all-purpose flour

2 cups (500 ml) milk

1 tbsp pistachio paste

3 thin sheets sponge cake

Syrup:

1 organic orange, **1** organic lemon

2 cups (500 ml) water

1 cup less 1 tbsp (6½ oz or 180 g) sugar

Remove the rinds from the organic orange and lemon for the syrup, and trim off the white pith. Place the rind in a small saucepan with the water and sugar and bring to a boil. Let simmer for 10 minutes then cool.

Beat the egg yolks in a bowl with the sugar for the millefeuille. Add the grated lemon zest and the flour. Bring the milk to a boil and pour in a thin stream onto the egg mixture, whisking constantly. Return to the heat and continue cooking and whisking until thickened. Transfer to a wide bowl and let cool.

Mix about 3 tablespoons of the cream with the pistachio paste. Transfer the remaining cream to a food processor or blender and blend to remove any lumps.

Brush the sponge cake with the citrus syrup. Place a layer on a sheet of parchment paper. Spread with half the pastry cream and cover with another layer of syrup-brushed cake. Press down firmly and evenly, then spread with the remaining pastry cream. Top with another layer of syrup-brushed cake, then decorate with the pistachio cream, using a pastry bag with a ridged tip. Refrigerate for 2 hours. Just before serving, cut into squares using a sharp knife.

Preparation time **20 minutes**
Cooking time **20 minutes**
Level **medium**

Simmering is the point just before a full boil, and is used to cook liquids and other foods which need a long, slow cooking time.

chestnut and honey squares
with foie gras

Ingredients for 4 servings

Squares:

3/4 cup plus 2 tbsps (5½ oz or 150 g) chestnut flour

salt and pepper

1 tbsp dark honey, such as chestnut

2 tbsps light extra-virgin olive oil

1 rosemary sprig, leaves only

7 oz (200 g) foie gras

1 tbsp raisins

1/2 tbsp Marsala wine

Preheat the oven to 400°F (200°C or Gas Mark 6).
Sift the chestnut flour and stir in enough water to make a light, fluid mixture. Season lightly with salt and pepper and stir in the honey and olive oil.
Pour into a lightly oiled non-stick rimmed baking sheet, making a thin layer. Sprinkle with rosemary leaves and bake for about 15 minutes.
Remove from the oven and cut into squares. Keep warm.
Cut the foie gras into cubes using a sharp knife.
Heat the knife over a flame to facilitate slicing.
Soak the raisins in the Marsala and a little water, then drain and squeeze out.
Place the foie gras cubes on top of the chestnut squares.
Garnish with raisins, adjust salt and pepper, and serve.

Did you know that Marsala wine has therapeutic properties? During the Prohibition era in the United States it was imported with a label stating "Hospital Size" and giving the recommended dose, "a small glassful twice a day."

Preparation time **15 minutes**
Cooking time **15 minutes**
Level **easy**

beignets with chantilly cream

Ingredients for 8 servings
Beignets:

4 eggs, **1** cup (250 ml) milk

6 tbsps (3 oz or 90 g) butter, salt

1 cup plus 3 tbsps (5½ oz or 150 g)
all-purpose flour

Cream:

4 egg yolks

2/3 cup (4 oz or 120 g) sugar

1/2 cup (2 oz or 60 g) all-purpose flour

2 cups (500 ml) milk, vanilla extract

1/3 cup (80 ml) heavy cream

Garnish:

pink glaze

To make a pink glaze at home, add a few drops of Alchermes liqueur or red food coloring and 1 tablespoon water to 2 cups (9 oz or 250 g) confectioners' sugar, stirring until it forms a liquid mixture. To make it thicker, add an egg white.

Preheat the oven to 400°F (200°C or Gas Mark 6).
Bring the milk for the beignets to a boil with the butter and a pinch of salt. Add the flour all at once and beat with a whisk. Continue to cook over low heat, stirring with a wooden spoon, until the mixture comes away from the sides of the pan. Transfer to a work surface or a wide bowl. As soon as the mixture has cooled, add the eggs one at a time, stirring with a wooden spoon, adding each egg only after the previous one has been incorporated.
Transfer the dough to a pastry bag with a smooth tip.
Pipe walnut-sized mounds onto baking sheet lined with parchment paper, about 1½ inches (3-4 cm) apart.
Bake for about 20 minutes, then let cool.
Meanwhile prepare the cream. Beat the egg yolks with the sugar. Add the flour. Bring the milk and vanilla to a boil and then pour over the egg yolk mixture, beating constantly. Return to the heat and continue cooking, whisking constantly, until thickened. Let cool.
Whip the cream and fold into the pastry cream.
Make a small hole in the base of the beignets and fill with the chantilly cream. Decorate the top with the pink glaze.

Preparation time **30 minutes**
Cooking time **40 minutes**
Level **medium**

ricotta and blueberry pastries

Ingredients for 4 servings
Pastries:
10½ oz (300 g) puff pastry
5½ oz (150 g) ricotta
seeds from **1** vanilla bean
2 tbsps sugar, zest of **1** organic lemon
1/2 basket blueberries, **1** egg, beaten
Blueberry sauce:
1/2 basket blueberries
2 tbsps water, **1** tbsp honey

Preheat the oven to 375°F (190°C or Gas Mark 5).
Roll out the puff pastry and cut it into 4 rectangles,
1½ inches by 3 inches (4 cm by 8 cm).
Beat the ricotta with the vanilla seeds, sugar and lemon
zest. Place the filling on half of each rectangle.
Add a few blueberries and fold in half.
Pinch the edges closed to seal.
Brush the pastries with the beaten egg.
Make a few diagonal incisions on the top of each pastry.
Bake for 20 minutes.
Meanwhile, heat the remaining blueberries with the water
and the honey. Once the berries are soft, remove from
heat and puree the sauce.
Serve the warm pastries with the blueberry sauce.

⌐ The blueberries could be replaced
by raspberries, pitted cherries or
even shavings of dark chocolate.

Preparation time **25 minutes**
Cooking time **25 minutes**
Level **easy**

cream puffs

Ingredients for 8 servings

Beignets:

1 cup (250 ml) water

7 tbsps (3½ oz or 100 g) butter, salt

1 cup plus **3** tbsps (5½ oz or 150 g) all-purpose flour

3 eggs

Cream:

1 vanilla bean, **2** cups (500 ml) milk

rind of **1** organic lemon, **4** egg yolks

2/3 cup (4 oz or 125 g) sugar, salt

6½ tbsps all-purpose flour

Garnish:

confectioners' sugar

To simplify this recipe, use good quality ready-made beignets instead of making them at home.

Prepare the beignets according to the recipe on page 296, using water instead of milk and only 3 eggs.
Open the vanilla bean lengthways and add to the milk together with the lemon rind. Cook over very low heat, without boiling, for about an hour.
Scrape the vanilla seeds into the milk and discard the bean and the lemon rind.
Beat the egg yolks with the sugar and a pinch of salt.
Add the flour and then pour in the hot milk.
Return to the heat, whisking constantly, and once thickened transfer to a bowl and let cool.
Fill the cooked beignets with the cooled cream.
Dust with confectioners' sugar and serve cold.

Preparation time **40 minutes**
Cooking time **35 minutes**
Level **medium**

barley arancini with cappuccino cream

Ingredients for 4 servings

Arancini:

1 cup (7 oz or 200 g) pearl barley

1 vanilla bean, **4** tbsps sugar

1¼ cups (300 ml) hot milk

2 oz (50 g) maritozzo
(sweet currant bread)

sunflower oil

Cream:

3 tbsps heavy cream, **1** tbsp sugar

1/4 cup (60 ml) prepared
espresso coffee

Garnish:

1 vanilla bean (optional)

Maritozzo is a sweet yeast bread from
Rome. During the 19th century it was
traditional for men to give the bread to
their fiancées during Lent. The name
derives from a word meaning "Lenten."
Today it is eaten year-round, usually cut
in half and filled with whipped cream.

Place the barley in a saucepan with the vanilla bean,
opened lengthwise, and cover with water. Bring to a boil.
Add the sugar. As soon as all the water has been
absorbed, add the hot milk. Remove from the heat
(the barley will still be al dente) and stir in the crumbled
maritozzo. Cover and let cool (this will complete
the cooking).
With damp hands, form the barley mixture into balls
about 1 inch (2 cm) in diameter. Refrigerate.
Partially whip the cream. Beat the coffee and sugar
together with a small whisk or a fork until creamy.
Heat the sunflower oil and fry the arancini.
Drain on paper towels.
Serve hot, accompanied by the cream with the sweetened
coffee poured over, garnished with a vanilla bean
if desired.

Preparation time **30 minutes**
Cooking time **35 minutes**
Level **easy**

dried vanilla-scented apples and pears

Ingredients for 4 servings
Dried Vanilla-Scented:

3 firm, ripe pears

2 Golden Delicious apples

juice of **1** lemon

3/4 cup (3½ oz or 100 g) confectioners' sugar

1 vanilla bean

Slice the pears into 3 thick slices, removing the core. Peel and core the apples and cut into 8 wedges each. Sprinkle lemon juice over the fruit.
Arrange on a baking sheet lined with parchment paper and sprinkle with confectioners' sugar.
Sprinkle over the vanilla bean and bake at 110°F (60°C) for 8-10 hours, leaving the oven door slightly ajar.

During the winter the fruit can be dried over the heat of a radiator or heater, covered with a breathable fabric which can keep them clean. This will take longer than in the oven. In the past fruit was strung up and hung out in the sun to dry.

Preparation time **10 minutes**
Cooking time **8 hours**
Level **easy**

vol-au-vents with yogurt cream and minted strawberries

Ingredients for 4 servings
Vol-au-Vents:

3/4 cup (7 oz or 200 g) low-fat yogurt

1 tbsp vanilla confectioners' sugar

3 tbsps heavy cream

1 basket strawberries, diced

1 tbsp sugar

1 fresh mint sprig, chopped

12 vol-au-vents

1 tsp sweetened cocoa powder

Mix together the yogurt and confectioners' sugar.
Whip the cream and fold into the sweetened yogurt.
Refrigerate.
Toss the strawberries with the sugar and mint.
Let sit for 30 minutes.
Fill the vol-au-vents with the yogurt cream
and strawberry mixture.
Dust with cocoa powder and serve.

To make vol-au-vents at home, cut out 24 circles of puff pastry using a serrated cookie cutter. Using a smaller cutter, cut out the centers of 12 of the circles. Lay them on top of the whole circles and brush with beaten egg. Bake for 20 minutes at 400°F (200°C or Gas Mark 6).

Preparation time **30 minutes**
Level **medium**

orange fritters

Ingredients for 4 servings
Fritters:

7 tbsps (3½ oz or 100 g) butter

4¾ cups (1⅓ lb or 600 g) all-purpose flour

1 tsp salt

1 tbsp sugar, plus extra for garnish

5 tbsps orange juice

3 tbsps iced water

sunflower oil

Mix together the butter and flour using two forks. When they are well mixed, add salt, sugar, orange juice and iced water and mix. Without touching the dough by hand, roll it out and fold over in half.
Repeat twice more, then place the dough in the freezer until very cold.
Roll the cold dough out very thinly and cut into diagonal strips. Make a cut in the center of each one.
Heat the sunflower oil and fry the dough strips, draining them on paper towels.
Sprinkle abundantly with sugar and serve hot.

The Italian word for flour, farina, derives from the Latin far, meaning farro, or emmer wheat, a grain which was much used in the past for flour production. Now the grain most used for flour is wheat.

Preparation time **30 minutes**
Cooking time **5 minutes**
Level **easy**

sweet coconut fritters

Ingredients for 4 servings
Fritters:

3 tbsps almonds, peeled

3 tbsps rice flour

2 tbsps finely ground semolina

1 cup (250 ml) rice milk

2 tbsps pistachios, finely chopped

4 tbsps shredded coconut

3 tbsps corn malt

1 tsp active dry yeast

1 pinch of saffron

peanut oil

Toast the almonds for 3 minutes in the oven, then mince them. Mix the rice flour, semolina and rice milk.
Add the minced almonds, pistachios, coconut flour and corn malt. Add the yeast and saffron.
Stir well, using a whisk, and let rest for 20 minutes.
Heat abundant peanut oil, then fry spoonfuls of the batter.
Drain and sprinkle with coconut flour, if desired.

Malt is produced from germinating grains (such as wheat, barley, rye or corn). Depending on how it is dried, malt can be used to make alcoholic beverages (beer or whisky), coffee substitutes and diet flours.

Preparation time **20 minutes**
Cooking time **15 minutes**
Level **easy**

wheat tarts with ricotta and lemon

Ingredients for 4 servings
Tarts:

2 tbsps (1 oz or 30 g) butter

1 egg, **2** tbsps sugar

1¼ cup (5½ oz or 150 g)
all-purpose flour

4 oz (120 g) cooked wheat

4½ tbsps milk

2 tbsps honey, peel of **1/2** lemon

3½ oz (100 g) ricotta

1/4 cup pine nuts

confectioners' sugar

Preheat the oven to 350°F (180°C or Gas Mark 4).
Melt the butter in a double boiler. Let cool.
Beat the egg and sugar together.
Add the butter and flour and mix until the dough
is smooth and elastic. Refrigerate for 30 minutes.
Heat the cooked wheat, milk, honey and lemon peel.
Simmer the mixture until the milk has been completely
absorbed by the wheat. Remove from the heat and let
cool. Remove the lemon peel and add the ricotta, mixing
with a wooden spoon.
Roll out the dough into a thin sheet and cut out 4 rounds.
Place the rounds on the bottom of 4 individual tart tins.
Use the remaining dough to cut out 4 strips.
Place the strips around the edges of the tins and press
down to seal the bottom and sides. Pour the cooked wheat
filling into the tarts and top with the pine nuts. Bake
for 25 minutes.
Sprinkle with confectioners' sugar before serving.

Cooking something over
a double boiler or bain-marie
means cooking over
a pot of boiling water.

Preparation time **40 minutes**
Cooking time **30 minutes**
Level **easy**

after-hours
Finger Foods

ricotta, pine nut and lemon rings

Ingredients for 4 servings

Rings:

7 oz (200 g) fresh ricotta

1/2 cup (3½ oz or 100 g) sugar

1/2 tsp vanilla extract

grated zest of **1** organic lemon

1 egg, **1** egg yolk

1 tbsp cornstarch

2 tbsps all-purpose flour

2 tbsps pine nuts

confectioners' sugar

lemon rind, julienned (optional)

Preheat the oven to 350°F (180°C or Gas Mark 4).
Beat the ricotta in a bowl with the sugar, vanilla extract and lemon zest. Stir in the egg, egg yolk, cornstarch and flour.
Toast the pine nuts in a non-stick frying pan.
Butter and flour 4 individual aluminum ring molds.
Divide the pine nuts between the molds. Pour in the ricotta mixture and level off the top. Bake for about 30 minutes, then let cool.
Unmold the rings, sprinkle with confectioners' sugar and garnish, if desired, with julienned lemon rind.

For an extra treat, fill the rings with a ball of vanilla ice cream just before serving.

Preparation time **20 minutes**
Cooking time **30 minutes**
Level **easy**

pistachio tart

Ingredients for 4 servings

Crust:

2/3 cup (5 oz or 140 g) butter

1/2 cup (70 g or 2½ oz) confectioners' sugar, **3** egg yolks

grated zest of **1** organic lemon

1/2 tsp baking soda, salt

1⅔ cups (7½ oz or 210 g) all-purpose flour

Filling:

4 egg yolks, **1** tbsp pistachio paste

1/2 cup (3½ oz or 100 g) sugar, salt

6½ tbsps all-purpose flour

2 cups (500 ml) milk

Garnish:

2 oz (60 g) dark chocolate

⌐ To speed up this recipe, use ready-made puff pastry instead of the homemade dough.

Beat the butter and confectioners' sugar in a bowl with an electric whisk until creamy. Add the egg yolks one at a time, then the lemon zest, baking soda and salt. Stir in the flour and mix quickly. Wrap the dough in plastic wrap and refrigerate for 1 hour. Preheat the oven to 325°F (170°C or Gas Mark 3). Beat the egg yolks for the filling with the sugar. Add a little salt and the sifted flour. Bring the milk to a boil and pour it over the egg yolks in a thin stream, beating constantly. Return to the heat and continue cooking until thickened. Stir in the pistachio paste and let cool. Butter and flour 4 small, round metal molds. Roll out the dough and use it to line the molds. Poke holes in the base with a fork and bake for 20 minutes. Unmold the tart crusts and let them cool. Fill with the pistachio cream. Melt the chocolate and use it to fill a cone made by rolling a triangle of parchment paper in the palm of the hand. Cut off the point and use it to drizzle melted chocolate over the surface of the tarts.

Preparation time **40 minutes**
Cooking time **35 minutes**
Level **medium**

banana-soy cakes
with strawberry sauce

Ingredients for 4 servings
Cakes:

1/2 cup (3½ oz or 100 g) soy yogurt

2 tbsps corn malt extract

3 tbsps sesame oil, **1** banana, peeled

3/4 cup plus 2 tbsps (3½ oz or 110 g)
whole-wheat flour

7½ tbsps all-purpose flour

1 tsp active dry yeast

Sauce:

1 basket strawberries, hulled

1 tbsp honey, **2** tbsps rice milk

Preheat the oven to 350°F (180°C or Gas Mark 4).
Puree the soy yogurt, corn malt extract, sesame oil
and banana in a food processor.
Mix together the two flours and add them to the yogurt
mixture little by little, stirring well. Add the yeast and
continue stirring until the mixture is soft and smooth.
Pour into individual molds and bake for 30 minutes.
Meanwhile puree the strawberries with the honey
and rice milk in a food processor.
Unmold the cakes and serve with the strawberry sauce.

The same recipe for the individual
cakes can be used to make
a single large cake. When it has
cooled, cut it in half and fill with
pieces of strawberry dressed
with the juice of 1 lemon and
1 tablespoon raw cane sugar.

Preparation time **20 minutes**
Cooking time **30 minutes**
Level **easy**

chocolate-dipped candied orange peel

Ingredients for 4 servings
Chocolate-Dipped:

7 oz (200 g) whole pieces of candied
orange peel
5½ oz (150 g) dark chocolate
or couverture, chopped

Cut the orange peel into large pieces or a thick julienne.
Melt two-thirds of the chocolate over a double boiler
or in the microwave at low power, stirring often.
Remove from the heat and stir in the remaining chocolate.
Continue stirring until melted.
Dip the orange peel into the chocolate. Tap off the excess,
then lay on a sheet of waxed paper. Once cooled
and hardened, serve.
They can also be stored in an airtight container or bag
for several days.

This simple but tasty recipe can be
enhanced by dipping the orange peel
first in chocolate and then
in some chopped hazelnuts.

Preparation time **45 minutes**
Cooking time **30 minutes**
Level **medium**

hazelnut and pumpkin-seed brittle

Ingredients for 4 servings

Hazelnut:

1¾ cups (10½ oz or 300 g) hazelnuts, skins removed (see note below)

1/2 cup (3½ oz or 100 g) raw cane sugar

1 tbsp water

1 cup (2 oz or 60 g) salted pumpkin seeds

Toast the hazelnuts in a non-stick frying pan. Add the sugar, and then shortly afterwards the water. Caramelize over low heat, stirring constantly, then add the pumpkin seeds when the sugar is dark brown and the hazelnuts completely glazed and shiny.

Transfer the mixture to a work surface covered in parchment paper and spread it out into a thin layer. Let cool 10 minutes, then break into pieces by hand and serve.

To remove the skins from hazelnuts, blanch them for 2 minutes in boiling water then drain. Dry them, then bake in a 320°F (160°C) oven for 15 minutes. Finally rub them well with a clean kitchen towel, and the skins should come off. This brittle can be wrapped in greaseproof paper and stored for several days.

Preparation time **25 minutes**
Cooking time **10 minutes**
Level **easy**

mini pineapple
and orange pies

Ingredients for 4 servings
Pies:

2 juicy oranges

2 tbsps raw cane sugar

2 cinnamon sticks

1/2 pineapple, peeled, cored and diced

10½ oz (300 g) shortcrust
pastry dough

9 oz (250 g) puff pastry

1 tab of butter, melted

confectioners' sugar

ground cinnamon (optional)

orange rind, julienned (optional)

Squeeze the oranges and strain the juice through a chinois sieve. Mix with the sugar in a saucepan, add the cinnamon sticks and bring to a boil. Remove from the heat, add the pineapple, and let sit for 1 hour.
Preheat the oven to 375°F (190°C or Gas Mark 5). Meanwhile roll the shortcrust pastry out to a thin layer on a floured work surface and use it to line 4 small, round, low-rimmed metal molds. Poke holes in the bottom with a fork. Drain the pineapple and divide between the molds. Roll the puff pastry out thinly and use it to top the pies, pressing down at the sides so that it sticks to the shortcrust pastry and rolling over with a rolling pin to trim the edges. Brush on a little melted butter and make cuts in the top to allow steam to escape.
Bake for about 25 minutes. Remove from the oven and let cool, then unmold.
Dust with confectioners' sugar and serve, garnished with a pinch of ground cinnamon and julienned orange rind, if desired.

Chinois sieves have an unmistakable funnel shape, and their name comes from the classic Chinese straw hats. Take care when using as they are quite fragile.

Preparazione **30 minuti**
Cottura **35 minuti**
Esecuzione **medium**

apple and cinnamon tartlets

Ingredients for 6 servings

Crust:

7 tbsps (3½ oz or 100 g) butter,
at room temperature

6 tbsps sugar, **1** pinch vanilla powder

1½ cups plus 1½ tbsps
(7 oz or 200 g) all-purpose flour

Filling:

2 yellow apples, peeled and chopped

1 tbsp pine nuts, finely chopped

1 tbsp raw cane sugar

Cream:

2 egg yolks, **1** tbsp cornstarch

3/4 cup plus 1 tbsp (200 ml) milk

5 tbsps raw cane sugar

1/2 tsp ground cinnamon

The apples can be replaced with the same number of pears, prepared in the same way. The tartlets could be topped with a few chocolate chips before baking.

Preheat the oven to 350°F (180°C or Gas Mark 4).
Cream the butter with the sugar for the crust. Add a pinch of vanilla, and gradually add the flour. Continue mixing to obtain a soft and compact dough.
Let rest for 10 minutes, then roll out with a rolling pin and use to line 6 individual tartlet tins.
Place the apples, pine nuts and raw cane sugar in a non-stick frying pan and cook over high heat for 5 minutes.
Meanwhile whisk together the egg yolks, milk and sugar, then add the cornstarch and cinnamon.
Divide the sautéed apple mixture between the tartlet tins and pour over the egg yolk mixture. Bake for 18 minutes.

Preparation time **30 minutes**
Cooking time **40 minutes**
Level **easy**

individual rice, lemon and almond puddings

Ingredients for 6 servings

Puddings:

1/2 cup (3½ oz or 100 g)
Originario rice

salt, **1** cup (250 ml) hot milk

zest of **1** organic lemon, 1/2 chopped
and 1/2 grated

1/3 cup (2 oz or 50 g) almonds

2/3 cup (4 oz or 120 g) sugar

2 tbsps (1 oz or 30 g) butter

1 tbsp all-purpose flour

3 eggs, separated

orange zest (optional)

Preheat the oven to 325°F (170°C or Gas Mark 3).
Boil the rice in lightly salted water for 20 minutes,
then drain. Transfer to a non-stick saucepan and cover
with hot milk. Add a few pieces of chopped lemon zest
and cook for 15 minutes, until the milk is completely
absorbed, stirring frequently.
Toast the almonds in a small frying pan, then puree
in a food processor until finely ground.
Stir 7½ tablespoons sugar, half the butter, the flour,
egg yolks and lemon zest into the rice.
Beat the egg whites into stiff peaks, then fold into
the rice mixture.
Butter 8 small pudding molds and sprinkle with sugar.
Fill with the batter and arrange in a deep-rimmed baking
dish. Pour about a cup (250 ml) of warm water into
the bottom of the dish, and bake for about 25 minutes.
Remove from the oven and let the puddings cool in the
water. Remove from the dish when cool and refrigerate
for 1 hour before unmolding and serving, decorated
with curls of orange zest, if desired.

Preparation time **30 minutes**
Cooking time **1 hour**
Level **easy**

Almond trees originated in Central
Asia, and they are now found widely
throughout the Mediterranean basin.
Almonds are a natural diet supplement,
combating weakness and depression.

glazed oranges

Ingredients for 4-6 servings
Glazed oranges:
3⅓ lb (1½ kg) thick-skinned oranges
1½ cups (300 ml) water
7¾ cups (3⅓ lb or 1½ kg) sugar
2 cinnamon sticks
juice of **1** lemon

Lightly grate the surface of the oranges to allow the oils to come out. Boil the whole oranges for about 20 minutes, until soft.
Drain and dry, then slice every orange into 8 wedges. Cut off the hard, central part with the seeds using scissors.
Heat the water and sugar until dissolved.
Add the orange wedges and cinnamon sticks and boil until thick and syrupy. Add the lemon juice, then after a few minutes remove from the heat.
Let cool, then pour into sterilized jars and seal.

332

Oranges come from an evergreen tree native to China and Japan, which can reach up to 30 feet 10 m) in height. Introduced to Italy by the Arabs in the 14th century, it produces fruits rich in citric acid, sugars, vitamins and minerals.

Preparation time **15 minutes**
Cooking time **35 minutes**
Level **easy**

apple and rice fritters

Ingredients for 4 servings
Fritters:

1 cup (200 g) brown rice

1 cup (250 ml) rice milk

1 cup (250 ml) water, salt

1/2 tsp vanilla extract

1/2 tsp ground cinnamon

grated zest of **1** organic lemon

5 tbsps corn malt, **2** eggs

3 apples, peeled, cored and chopped

sesame oil

2 tbsps shredded coconut

Cook the rice in the rice milk and water for 30 minutes.
Add a pinch of salt, the vanilla, cinnamon and grated
lemon zest and let the mixture sit for 20 minutes.
Stir in the malt, eggs and apples.
Heat the sesame oil until very hot. Fry spoonfuls
of the rice mixture in the hot oil until golden, then drain
and sprinkle with shredded coconut before serving.

This delicious recipe is perfect for
anyone who is lactose intolerant.
Rice milk is lactose-free and very
digestible, as well as being
low in fat and cholesterol.

Preparation time **40 minutes**
Cooking time **20 minutes**
Level **easy**

lemon madeleines

Ingredients for 4 servings
Madeleines:

1 cup (8 oz or 225 g) butter, chopped

4 eggs

1 cup plus 3½ tbsps
(8 oz or 230 g) sugar

2 cups plus 2½ tbsps (10 oz or 275 g)
all-purpose flour

2¼ tsps active dry yeast

grated zest of **1** organic lemon

Melt the butter in a microwave or over a double boiler. As soon as it is liquid, remove from the heat and let cool completely.
Meanwhile beat the eggs with the sugar until foamy and pale yellow, using a whisk or an electric beater.
Sift the flour and yeast together and fold into the egg mixture, together with the lemon zest. Let rest for 1 hour at room temperature.
Spoon off the white cream formed on the butter and add the rest to the dough, carefully pouring it in but stopping before reaching the final watery, whitish part. Mix well and let sit in a cool place for 30 minutes.
Preheat the oven to 475°F (240°C or Gas Mark 9).
Butter and flour a madeleine mold, ideally made of silicon, and fill with spoonfuls of the mixture.
Bake for about 8 minutes, then unmold and set on a wire rack to dry and cool.

Madeleines are a typical French sweet, made famous by Marcel Proust, who in Remembrance of Things Past associated their taste with the memory of happy childhood moments.

Preparation time **30 minutes**
Cooking time **10 minutes**
Level **easy**

chocolate and coconut truffles

Ingredients for 4 servings
Truffles:

7 oz (200 g) milk chocolate, chopped

4½ tbsps heavy cream

1 tsp unsweetened cocoa powder

1/2 cup (2 oz or 60 g) finely chopped hazelnuts

1¾ cups (5½ oz or 150 g) shredded coconut

Place the chocolate and cream in a heat-proof glass bowl. Melt over a double boiler, stirring often with a wooden spoon. As soon as the mixture is smooth, remove from the heat. Stir in the cocoa powder and hazelnuts.
Let cool until it reaches a moldable consistency.
Form the mixture into walnut-sized balls by rolling a spoonful between the hands, then roll them in the shredded coconut.
Refrigerate the truffles for a few hours before serving.

Make sure not to let any water drip into the chocolate mixture while melting, because it will make it crystallize. Alternatively use a microwave on medium power, stirring the mixture frequently.

Preparation time **15 minutes**
Cooking time **5 minutes**
Level **easy**

yogurt and raspberry muffins

Ingredients for 8 servings

Muffins:

2 eggs, **3** tbsps raw cane sugar

1 tsp vanilla extract

grated zest of **1** organic lemon

1 cup (9 oz or 250 g) yogurt

3 tbsps corn oil, **1** basket raspberries

3/4 cup (3½ oz or 100 g)
all-purpose flour

6½ tbsps emmer wheat flour

1 tsp active dry yeast, butter

confectioners' sugar (optional)

Preheat the oven to 350°F (180°C or Gas Mark 4).
Whisk the eggs and sugar together. Add the vanilla,
lemon zest, yogurt and corn oil and mix well. Lightly flour
the raspberries.
Add the all-purpose flour, emmer flour and yeast
to the egg mixture and then stir in the raspberries.
Butter and flour miniature muffin molds, then fill with
the batter. Bake for 25 minutes.
Remove from the oven and let cool slightly. Serve, still
warm, dusted with confectioners' sugar if desired.

Raspberries are harvested in the early
hours of the day and then immediately
chilled, as they are one of the most
delicate fruits and very sensitive to high
temperatures. They can be stored
in the refrigerator for 1-2 days.

Preparation time **15 minutes**
Cooking time **25 minutes**
Level **easy**

apple and cinnamon fritters

Ingredients for 4 servings

Fritters:

1¼ cups (5½ oz or 160 g)
all-purpose flour

1/2 cup (3½ oz or 100 g) sugar

salt

4 eggs, **7** tbsps milk

1/3 cup (80 ml) beer

3½ tbsps (2 oz or 50 g) butter

3 apples, sliced

1/2 tsp ground cinnamon

sunflower oil

Sift the flour together with 2 teaspoons of sugar and a pinch of salt.
Beat the eggs and milk together, then gradually mix into the flour. Add the beer and continue mixing until smooth.
Heat the butter and 1 tablespoon sugar in a non-stick frying pan and add the apple slices. Sauté until tender and caramelized. Add the apples to the batter, adding extra flour if it is too liquid.
Mix the cinnamon with 2 tablespoons of sugar.
Heat the sunflower oil in a frying pan and fry spoonfuls of the apple batter until puffy and golden. Drain on paper towels and dip in the cinnamon sugar. Serve immediately.

It is important to know the origin of apples, to make sure they are not being grown with the use of too many chemicals. Organic apples are a good idea, or apples from a known brand, while anonymous apples, particularly out of season, are hard to trust.

Preparation time **20 minutes**
Cooking time **15 minutes**
Level **easy**

sicilian almond brittle

Ingredients for 4 servings
Almond:
2½ cups (9 oz or 250 g) sliced almonds

1 tbsp peanut oil

2/3 cup (4 oz or 120 g) sugar

1/2 tsp glucose (optional)

3/4 cup (3½ oz or 100 g) pistachios, finely chopped

Preheat the oven to 400°F (200°C or Gas Mark 6).
Toast the almonds in the oven for about 4 minutes, turning often so they don't get too brown.
Oil a sheet of parchment paper with the peanut oil.
Heat the sugar, glucose (if using) and 1 tablespoon water in a saucepan. Let caramelize gently until a dark blonde color, then add half the almonds. Immediately transfer to the oiled parchment paper and spread out with a spatula. Cover with the rest of the almonds and the pistachios.
Lay over a second sheet of parchment paper and press down. Let cool.
Cut the brittle into squares, and store in an air-tight container.

Pistachios can be stored for up to 6 months in a fresh, dry, dark place, closed in plastic bags or air-tight containers to avoid them developing an unpleasant odor.

Preparation time **15 minutes**
Cooking time **15 minutes**
Level **easy**

almond pastries

Ingredients for 4 servings

Dough:

2⅓ cups (10½ oz or 300 g) all-purpose flour

1 egg

2 tbsps (1 oz or 30 g) melted butter

grated zest of **1** organic lemon

Filling:

2 cups (10½ oz or 300 g) peeled almonds

1 cup minus 1 tbsp (6½ oz or 180 g) sugar

7 tbsps (3½ oz or 100 g) butter, chopped

3 tsps orange-flower water

Topping:

2 cu1 egg white, beaten

3 tbsps confectioners' sugar

⌐ The almond filling could be replaced by a chocolate cream or a fruit jam.

Puree the almonds with the sugar, butter and orange-flower water in a food processor, to obtain a coarse, soft mixture.

Mound the flour on a work surface and make a well in the center. Add the egg, melted butter and lemon zest, and mix together using the finger tips. Continue kneading using the palm of the hand until the dough is elastic, then wrap in plastic wrap and refrigerate for 30 minutes. Preheat the oven to 325°F (170°C or Gas Mark 3).

Roll the dough out thinly and cut into oval shapes using a rolling cutter or a sharp knife. Place a lump of the almond mixture in the middle of each one, then gently close over the two halves without pressing down to seal them.

Brush them with egg white and sprinkle with confectioners' sugar. Bake for about 20 minutes.

Preparation time **15 minutes**
Cooking time **20 minutes**
Level **easy**

sweet plum-filled tortelli

Ingredients for 4 servings

Tortelli:

7 tbsps (3½ oz or 100 g) butter

3/4 cup (3 oz or 90 g)
confectioners' sugar

1 egg

2⅓ cups (10½ oz or 300 g)
all-purpose flour

grated zest of **1** organic lemon

grated zest of **1** organic orange

4 tbsps plum jam

1 tbsp sugar

Preheat the oven to 320°F (160°C or Gas Mark 3).
Cream the butter and confectioners' sugar together,
then mix in the egg. Sift the flour and add to the mixture,
stirring with a wooden spoon.
Continue to stir, then add the lemon and orange zests.
Mix until smooth, then chill in the refrigerator.
Roll the dough out on a floured work surface and cut out
4 circles of 2½ inches (7 cm) in diameter, using a scalloped
cookie cutter. Place 1 tablespoon of jam on each circle and
fold over, pressing around the edges to seal.
Place on a baking sheet lined with parchment paper
and sprinkle with sugar.
Bake for about 15 minutes. Serve cooled, perhaps
with a cup of tea.

The filling could be changed, and
the plum jam replaced by blueberry
or apricot jam, or a hazelnut paste.

Preparation time **20 minutes**
Cooking time **15 minutes**
Level **medium**

cookies

Finger Foods

salted butter cookies

Ingredients for 4 servings

Cookies:

1/3 cup (2 oz or 50 g) pine nuts

4 tbsps sugar

3/4 cup (7 oz or 200 g) lightly salted butter, softened

3/4 cup plus 1½ tbsps (3½ oz or 100 g) confectioners' sugar

1 tsp vanilla extract

3 egg yolks

2 cups (9 oz or 250 g) all-purpose flour

Grind the pine nuts and sugar together in a food processor. Cream the butter with the confectioners' sugar and vanilla. Add the egg yolks and pine nut mixture and sift in the flour. Mix together as quickly as possible, then refrigerate for 2 hours.
Preheat the oven to 325°F (170°C or Gas Mark 3).
Roll the dough out quite thickly (about 1/3 inch or 8 mm) and cut out strips using a smooth rolling cutter or sharp knife. Cut the strips into narrow, long rectangles.
Poke holes in the top with a toothpick or a fork, and bake for about 15 minutes. Cool before serving.

Pine nuts have a high nutritional value. They are about 40% fat, with an average of 600 calories per 3½ oz (100 g). Additionally, thanks to their high iron content, they are recommended for sufferers of anemia.

Preparation time **15 minutes**
Cooking time **15 minutes**
Level **easy**

cherry bull's eyes

Ingredients for 4 servings

Bull's Eyes:

4 eggs

2 cups (9 oz or 250 g) all-purpose flour

3 tbsps rice flour

1/2 cup (4½ oz or 130 g) butter, chopped

2/3 cup (4½ oz or 130 g) sugar

1 tsp vanilla extract

grated zest of **1** organic lemon

salt, milk

5 tbsps cherry jam

Hard-boil 3 eggs. Let cool, then shell them and separate the yolks and whites. Discard the whites, and pass the yolks through a sieve.

Mound the all-purpose flour and rice flour on a work surface and make a hollow in the middle.

Add the chopped butter, sugar, vanilla, lemon zest, cooked egg yolks, remaining whole egg and a pinch of salt.

Mix together to form a smooth dough.

Wrap in plastic wrap and refrigerate for about 30 minutes.

Preheat the oven to 325°F (170°C or Gas Mark 3).

Roll the dough out thinly and cut out cookies using a round, smooth cookie cutter. Using a second, smaller cookie cutter, cut out the center of half the cookies.

Top the other half with the rings obtained, and arrange on a baking sheet lined with parchment paper.

Brush with a little milk and bake for 12 minutes.

Let cool. Heat the cherry jam, then use it fill the centers of the cookies. Let cool again before serving.

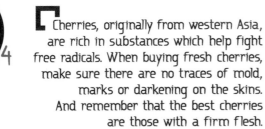

Cherries, originally from western Asia, are rich in substances which help fight free radicals. When buying fresh cherries, make sure there are no traces of mold, marks or darkening on the skins. And remember that the best cherries are those with a firm flesh.

Preparation time **15 minutes**
Cooking time **20 minutes**
Level **medium**

almond biscottini

Ingredients for 4 servings
Biscottini:

1/3 cup (3 oz or 85 g) butter, softened

1/2 cup (120 ml) agave juice

1 tsp ground cinnamon

1/2 tsp grated nutmeg

1 cup (4 oz or 120 g) finely chopped almonds

3 oz (80 g) citrus zest, **2** egg yolks

2¾ cups plus 1 tbsp (12½ oz or 350 g) all-purpose flour

1/2 packet active dry yeast

20 whole peeled almonds

1 egg white, beaten

Preheat the oven to 350°F (180°C or Gas Mark 4).
Mix together the butter and agave juice. Add the cinnamon, nutmeg, chopped almonds, citrus zest and egg yolks. Add the flour and yeast and mix together quickly into a dough. Wrap in plastic wrap and let sit for 10 minutes. Form the dough into small, walnut-sized balls.
Place an almond on top of each one and brush with egg white. Bake for 18 minutes. Remove from the oven and let cool on a wire rack before serving.

Agave is a plant whose name comes from the Greek term agauós, meaning "marvelous." A sugary juice is extracted from various species found in Mexico and the Yucatán and used to make the famous spirit tequila.

Preparation time **20 minutes**
Cooking time **18 minutes**
Level **easy**

caramel sandwich cookies

Ingredients for 4 servings
Cookies:

3 cups plus 3 tbsps (14 oz or 400 g)
all-purpose flour

1⅔ cups (7 oz or 200 g) cornstarch

3/4 cup plus 1½ tbsps (3½ oz or
100 g) confectioners' sugar

6½ tbsps (3½ oz or 100 g)
salted butter

1 egg, extra-virgin olive oil

1 large tin sweetened condensed milk

5½ tbsps unsweetened cocoa powder

Sift the flour, cornstarch and confectioners' sugar together into a bowl. Mix in the butter, then the egg, and continue mixing until it forms a soft dough. Let rest for 15 minutes. Preheat the oven to 350°F (180°C or Gas Mark 4).
Line a baking sheet with parchment paper and oil it with extra-virgin olive oil. Divide the dough into 4 pieces. Sprinkle flour on a work surface and roll out a piece of dough with a rolling pin to a thickness of about 1/10-inch (3 mm). Cut out disks using a round cookie cutter and arrange them on the baking sheet. Repeat with the other pieces of dough.
Bake for about 12-15 minutes, then leave to dry for 4 hours. Meanwhile place the tin of condensed milk in a saucepan and cover with water.
Bring to a boil and let boil for 3 hours. Drain the water, open the tin and mix the contents with the cocoa powder. Spread a small amount of the chocolate caramel on a cookie, then top with another one. Continue until all the cookies have been used up. Serve.

This kind of caramel is called dulce de leche, "milk candy," in Spanish, and is popular across Latin America.

Preparation time **30 minutes**
Cooking time **3 hours**
Level **easy**

apple and szechuan pepper horseshoes

Ingredients for 4 servings

Horseshoes:

3/4 cup (5½ oz or 150 g) sugar

2 cups (500 ml) water

1 tbsp acacia honey

1 ripe Golden Delicious apple, peeled and diced

1 pinch Szechwan pepper

1/2 cup (2 oz or 60 g) breadcrumbs

ground cinnamon, salt

1/4 cup (1 oz or 30 g) unpeeled almonds, finely chopped

warm milk (optional)

4 tbsps slivered almonds

Preheat the oven to 400°F (200°C or Gas Mark 6).
Place the sugar in a saucepan with the water and honey and bring to a boil. Continue cooking until the mixture starts to caramelize. Add the diced apple and cook for 2 minutes. Add the Szechwan pepper, breadcrumbs, a pinch of cinnamon, salt and chopped almonds. Transfer to a work surface. Knead the mixture, adding a little warm milk if necessary to soften it.
Form the dough into many small little sticks, then bend them into U shapes.
Dip into the slivered almonds, arrange on a baking sheet lined with parchment paper and bake for 15 minutes.

Szechwan pepper comes in brownish-red grains, and has a much stronger flavor and more fragrance than common black pepper.

Preparation time **10 minutes**
Cooking time **30 minutes**
Level **easy**

grape jelly cookies

Ingredients for 4-6 servings

Cookies:

4 eggs

2 cups (9 oz or 250 g) all-purpose flour

1/2 cup (4 oz or 125 g) butter

2/3 cup (4½ oz or 130 g) sugar

1 tsp vanilla extract

grated zest of **1** organic orange, salt

Jelly:

1 small bunch of grapes

1 tbsp sugar

1/2 cup (120 ml) Brachetto wine

1 gelatin sheet

Brachetto is a sweet, sparkling red wine from Italy's northeastern Piedmont region, with a heady fragrance that recalls roses and raspberries.

Hard-boil 3 eggs. Let cool, then shell them and separate the yolks and whites. Discard the whites, and pass the yolks through a sieve. Mound the flour on a work surface. Make a hollow in the middle and place the butter and sugar there. Break in the egg, then add the cooked egg yolks, vanilla, grated orange zest and a pinch of salt. Mix together quickly to form a dough. As soon as it is smooth, wrap in plastic wrap and refrigerate for 1 hour. Preheat the oven to 325°F (170°C or Gas Mark 3).
Crush the grapes in a small saucepan with the sugar and bring to a boil. Add the Brachetto and let reduce over low heat. Lightly puree the mixture with a hand-held immersion blender and strain through a wide-meshed sieve to remove the skins and seeds.
Soak the gelatin sheet until soft, squeeze out excess liquid then add to the grape mixture. Let cool.
Roll the dough out on a floured work surface and cut out circles with a fluted cookie cutter. Cut out smaller circles from the center of half the cookies, then place them on top of the other half. Bake for about 15 minutes, then let cool. Fill the cookies with the jelly, then let cool and harden.

Preparation time **30 minutes**
Cooking time **25 minutes**
Level **medium**

malted cumin cookies

Ingredients for 4 servings

Cookies:

1½ cups plus 1½ tbsps (7 oz or 200 g) all-purpose flour

4½ tbsps (2½ oz or 70 g) butter, softened and cut into pieces

1 tbsp sunflower oil

3 tbsps barley or corn malt extract

1 tsp ground cumin

2 tsps active dry yeast

salt

milk

confectioners' sugar

Place the flour in a bowl and add the butter, sunflower oil, malt extract, cumin, yeast and a pinch of salt. Mix together quickly, then wrap in plastic wrap and refrigerate for 30 minutes.
Preheat the oven to 350°F (180°C or Gas Mark 4).
Form the dough into thin ropes, then cut them into pieces 1½ inches (4 cm) long. Roll them around a finger and close, overlapping the two ends and pressing lightly with the fingers.
Arrange on a baking sheet lined with parchment paper, brush with milk and bake for 12 minutes. Sprinkle with a little confectioners' sugar and serve.

Cumin, as well as being a excellent seasoning, was also popularly believed to increase the milk production of wet-nurses.

Preparation time **20 minutes**
Cooking time **12 minutes**
Level **easy**

almond and cherry petits fours

Ingredients for 4 servings
Petits Fours:

(5½ oz or 150 g) almond flour

1¼ cups (5½ oz or 150 g) confectioners' sugar

1/3 oz (10 g) glucose

2 egg whites

salt

candied cherries
(or other candied fruit)

apricot jelly (or other clear fruit jelly)

Place the almond flour, confectioners' sugar, glucose, egg whites and salt in a bowl and mix quickly with a whisk or an electric beater until the mixture is smooth and viscous. Transfer to a pastry bag with a ridged tip and form large tufts on a baking sheet lined with greaseproof paper. Place a candied cherry on top of each one, then let them dry out overnight.
Preheat the oven to 485°F (250°C or Gas Mark 10).
Bake the petits fours for 2 minutes. Let cool.
Heat up the apricot jelly and brush the petits fours with it. Let cool then serve.

Petit four, literally "small oven", is the French name for these small little pastries, often served as part of an afternoon tea. They can come in many different shapes and use many different ingredients.

Preparation time **15 minutes**
Cooking time **2 minutes**
Level **medium**

lemon-cornmeal cookies

Ingredients for 4 servings
Cookies:

1 cup (5½ oz or 150 g) very finely ground cornmeal

1 cup plus 3 tbsps (5½ oz or 150 g) all-purpose flour

1/2 cup plus 2½ tbsps (5½ oz or 150 g) butter

3/4 cup (5½ oz or 150 g) sugar

grated zest of **1** organic lemon

2 tsps active dry yeast

3 tbsps milk, **1** egg

1 egg yolk, salt, confectioners' sugar

Lemons are the third most cultivated citrus fruits in Italy, after oranges and clementines. The trees bear fruit after 4 or 5 years, and produce between 200 and 600 fruit at a time. Rich in citric acid and vitamin C, lemons can be used as an astringent and thirst-quencher.

Mix together the cornmeal, flour, butter, sugar (reserving 2 tablespoons), grated lemon zest, yeast, milk, egg, egg yolk and salt quickly to form a soft dough. Form it into a ball, wrap in plastic wrap and let rest in the refrigerator for 30 minutes.

Preheat the oven to 350°F (180°C or Gas Mark 4).

Roll the dough out with a rolling pin and cut into several different shapes. Arrange on a buttered baking sheet and sprinkle with the reserved sugar. Bake for 15-20 minutes. When the cookies are golden, remove from the oven and let cool. Sprinkle with confectioners' sugar and serve.

Preparation time **20 minutes**
Cooking time **15 minutes**
Level **easy**

almond cookies

Makes 25 cookies

Cookies:

1 egg, **3** egg yolks

1½ cups (10½ oz or 300 g) sugar,
plus extra for sprinkling

2¼ cups (14 oz or 400 g) peeled,
almonds, finely chopped

10 drops orange-flower water

2 tbsps (1 oz or 30 g) melted butter

grated zest of **2** organic lemons

1/2 packet active dry yeast

Beat the whole egg and the yolks with half the sugar. Separately, mix the chopped almonds with the remaining sugar. Add the orange-flower water and blend in a food processor. Mix the almond mixture with the melted butter and grated lemon zest, then stir in the egg mixture little by little, to obtain a soft, malleable dough. Let rest for at least 2 hours.

Preheat the oven to 350°F (180°C or Gas Mark 4).

Mix the yeast into the dough. Oil hands with butter and form the dough into small, walnut-sized balls. Arrange them on a baking sheet and press down to flatten slightly. Sprinkle the tops with a little sugar and bake for 15-20 minutes.

There are two categories of yeast. Fresh yeasts are organisms which can work only in the presence of sugar. Chemical yeasts, on the other hand, react with water to create a chemical reaction which leads to leavening.

Preparation time **20 minutes**
Cooking time **20 minutes**
Level **easy**

brutti ma buoni

Ingredients for 4 servings
Brutti ma buoni:

2/3 cup (3½ oz or 100 g) almonds

3 tbsps Passito di Pantelleria wine

2/3 cup (3 oz or 80 g) confectioners' sugar

1 egg white

salt

2 tbsps sugar

1 tbsp cornstarch

Preheat the oven to 250°F (130°C or Gas Mark 1/2). Toast the almonds. Roughly chop two-thirds of them. Mix together the chopped almonds, wine, confectioners' sugar and the remaining whole almonds.
Beat the egg white with a pinch of salt until it forms soft peaks. Add the sugar, almond mixture and cornstarch and mix together gently.
Line a baking sheet with greaseproof paper. Drop spoonfuls of the batter on top, leaving about 1-inch (2 cm) between each spoonful.
Bake for about 40 minutes. Let cool before serving.

The name brutti ma buoni means "ugly but beautiful". Passito wine is a type of sweet dessert wine, produced by the Phoenicians in the 9th century BC as well as the ancient Romans. Passito di Pantelleria is from the tiny Sicilian island of the same name.

Preparation time **15 minutes**
Cooking time **40 minutes**
Level **easy**

raisin biscotti

Ingredients for 4 servings

Biscotti:

2/3 cup (3½ oz or 100 g) raisins

5 tsps (2/3 oz or 20 g)
active dry yeast

1/4 cup (60 ml) warm milk

2/3 cup (4 oz or 120 g) sugar

3 cups plus 3 tbsps (14 oz or 400 g)
all-purpose flour

6½ tbsps (3½ oz or 100 g)
butter, softened

salt

1½ tbsps aniseeds, **2** eggs

Soak the raisins in warm water. Dissolve the yeast in the warm milk. Add 3½ tablespoons sugar and enough flour to make a soft dough. Let rise for 20 minutes.
Drain the raisins and squeeze out any excess water. Mound the remaining flour on a work surface and make a hollow in the middle. Place the remaining sugar, raisins, butter, a pinch of salt, aniseeds and 1 egg in the center. Mix together until smooth. Add the already risen dough and continue kneading for another 10 minutes, until the dough is elastic. Let rise for 20 minutes. Divide the dough into 3 portions, and shape them into loaves. Make a cut on the surface of each one, and let rise for another 30 minutes.
Preheat the oven to 350°F (180°C or Gas Mark 4). Beat the remaining egg. Brush the tops of the loaves with the beaten egg and bake for 45-50 minutes. Let the loaves cool, then cut them into thin slices.
Lay them on the racks of the still-warm oven (about 210°F or 100°C) for 15 minutes to dry out.

Aniseeds, with their distinctive licorice flavor, are excellent with fruit and in salads, or in meat dishes. They can be replaced by fennel or dill seeds.

Preparation time **25 minutes**
Cooking time **1 hour 5 minutes**
Level **medium**

Cookies

hazelnut and white chocolate horseshoes

Ingredients for 8 servings

Horseshoes:

1/2 cup (2 oz or 60 g) peeled hazelnuts

3/4 cup plus 1½ tbsps (5½ oz or 160 g) sugar

1⅓ cups (8 oz or 220g) very finely ground cornmeal

1½ cups plus 1½ tbsps (7 oz or 200 g) all-purpose flour

1 cup plus 2 tbsps (10 oz or 280 g) butter

1 tsp vanilla extract, **4** eggs

3 oz (80 g) white chocolate, melted

This is a revisitation of a classic Piedmontese cookie, called crumiro. Traditionally the dough is piped using a pastry bag with a ridged tip. Once cooked, they are stored in tins for about 2 weeks.

Grind the hazelnuts and sugar in a food processor. Mix together the cornmeal and all-purpose flour in a bowl. Add the butter, either chopped into pieces or shaved with a vegetable peeler.

Add the hazelnut mixture, vanilla and eggs and mix together. Transfer to a work surface as soon as it starts to come together, and continue kneading with the palm of the hand. Wrap in plastic wrap and let rest in a cool place for 30 minutes.

Preheat the oven to 375°F (190°C or Gas Mark 5). Form the dough into many ropes, rolled out on a floured work surface. Cut the ropes into 3-inch (7-8 cm) lengths. Lay them on baking sheet lined with parchment paper and bend them into horseshoe shapes.

Bake for about 20 minutes. Remove from the oven, let cool, and then drizzle with melted white chocolate.

Preparation time **30 minutes**
Cooking time **20 minutes**
Level **easy**

candied ginger cookies

Ingredients for 4 servings
Cookies:

4 cups (1 lb plus 1½ oz or 500 g) all-purpose flour

3 eggs

3/4 cup (5½ oz or 150 g) sugar

6½ tbsps (3½ oz or 100 g) butter, chopped

1 tsp active dry yeast, salt

grated zest of **1** organic lemon

2 tbsps sweetened condensed milk

2 oz (50 g) candied ginger, finely chopped

How can ginger be preserved? The fresh root tends to deteriorate quickly. Try either storing the whole root in a jar of sand, or freezing it. Both ways seem to work quite well.

Mound the flour on a work surface and make a hollow in the middle. Break the eggs into it, reserving 1 egg white. Add the sugar (reserving 1 tablespoon), butter, yeast and a pinch of salt. Mix together with the fingertips, then add the grated lemon zest and condensed milk. Mix in, then add the candied ginger.
Work the dough until smooth, then wrap in plastic wrap and refrigerate for 20 minutes.
Preheat the oven to 210°F (100°C or Gas Mark 1/4).
Roll the dough out to a thickness of 1/5 inch (1/2 cm) and cut out large, rectangular shapes.
Arrange on a baking sheet lined with parchment paper. Beat together the remaining egg white and tablespoon of sugar, then brush the cookies with the mixture.
Bake for 15-20 minutes, let cool and then serve.

Preparation time **15 minutes**
Cooking time **20 minutes**
Level **easy**

basic tecniques

Finger Foods

BASIC RECIPES

Here are some basic recipes which are invaluable in the preparation of both savory and sweet finger foods.

Puff Pastry

Puff pastry is the base for many different preparations. It is light and crispy, and can be used with both sweet and savory ingredients.

Ingredients
1½ cups plus **1½** tbsps (7 oz or 200 g) all-purpose flour; **7** tbsps (100 ml) water; salt; **1** cup (9 oz or 250 g) margarine, cut into small pieces

Method
Mound the flour on a work surface, make a well in the middle, then add water and a pinch of salt. Mix together until smooth, then wrap in a clean kitchen towel and let rest for 20 minutes.

Roll the dough out with a rolling pin to 1/5-inch (1/2 cm) thick, then cut out a large square. Place the margarine in the middle, fold over the dough and close it completely, forming a parcel.

Roll out gently with the rolling pin, then wrap the dough in foil and refrigerate for 5 minutes.

Unwrap the dough and place on the work surface. Roll it out into a long strip (about 1/2 inch or 1 cm thick). Fold a third in towards the middle, then cover it with another third, to form three layers of dough. Turn it around 90 degrees, then roll the dough out again into a long strip.

Fold it again in thirds, then wrap in foil and refrigerate for about 30 minutes. Repeat two more times. When completed, leave the dough to rest in the

a word of advice...
Before baking puff pastry, make sure to make some cuts or holes in the pastry to allow steam to escape and avoid dampening the pastry.

Basic Tecniques

refrigerator for at least an hour before using. To make a good pastry, it is important to have all the ingredients at the same temperature, particularly the margarine. If it is too hard, it might break, and if it is too soft it might melt and run out. To give the finished pastry a golden sheen, brush with a beaten egg or some milk before baking.

Puff pastry is one of the most versatile doughs, because it is so adaptable to sweet and savory dishes. For appetizers and desserts, we recommend using it to create cannoli or other small containers for mousses and savory creams, to make vol-au-vents, for small napoleons of vegetables and béchamel, for savory strudels, to cover vegetable tarts, or simply rolled out, seasoned, cut into shapes and baked to make crunchy crackers to pair with salsas or creams.

Savory Pie Crust

This is a savory shortcrust, and can be used as a crust for pies, tartlets, small parcels or other shapes to be filled and baked. Usually it is brushed with beaten egg or milk before baking. It can be enriched by sprinkling with sesame, poppy or other seeds to give crunch and color.

Ingredients

2⅓ cups plus 1 tbsp (10½ oz or 300 g) all-purpose flour; salt; **1** egg; **5** tbsps (2½ oz or 70 g) butter; **1** tbsp extra-virgin olive oil

Method

Mound the flour on a work surface and make a well at the center. Add a pinch of salt and then the egg and olive oil. Mix to form a smooth dough. Cover with plastic wrap and refrigerate at least 30 minutes. This step is very important as it allows the ingredients to blend together fully. This dough can be used for

When making puff pastry do not replace the margarine with butter, as the latter contains very little water and so, unlike margarine, doesn't release steam during baking, helping puff up the pastry.

Basic Tecniques

crusts for savory tarts and quiches, remembering to poke holes in the base so it doesn't puff up during cooking and ruin the dish.

The dough can be refrigerated for a couple of days, wrapped in aluminum foil. Alternatively it can be frozen. Defrost slowly before use.

Beignets

Beignets can be filled and glazed with a whole range of ingredients, depending on taste. Often beignets are used as part of larger pastry constructions, functioning as very tasty building blocks and decorations (the mythical Saint-Honoré comes to mind).

One of the most popular uses for beignets is to make profiteroles. The batter used for beignets is very light and delicate, and can be used not only for confectionery but also for savory preparations such as small appetizers.

Ingredients for 4 servings
1 cup (250 ml) milk; **1/3** cup (3½ oz or 90 g) butter; **4** eggs; **1** cup plus **3** tbsps (5½ oz or 150 g) all-purpose flour; salt

Method
Preheat the oven to 400°F (200°C or Gas Mark 6). Bring the milk to a boil with a pinch of salt and the butter. Add the flour all at once and quickly beat vigorously with a whisk. Continue to cook over low heat, stirring with a wooden spoon, until the mixture comes away from the sides of the pan. Turn out onto a work surface or into a large bowl.

As soon as the mixture has cooled, stir in the eggs, one at a time, stirring with a wooden spoon and only adding the next egg after the first one is fully incorporated. Transfer the batter to a pastry bag with a smooth tip and form a

a secret...
It is important to use butter and eggs at room temperature and to work the dough quickly so the butter doesn't overheat, which could lead to a less elastic dough.

number of walnut-sized puffs on a baking sheet lined with parchment paper, at least 1½ inches (3-4 cm) apart. Bake for about 20 minutes and then cool.

Sweet Tartlet Dough

Puff pastry or shortcrust can be used for tartlets, rolled very thinly. Cut out the shapes desired with a cookie cutter, then use them to line buttered molds (usually round ones). Poke holes in the base to avoid puffing up during cooking. Line with parchment paper and fill with dried beans, then bake on a baking sheet for the necessary time. Remove the parchment paper and beans, brush with an egg yolk and water mixture, let dry, and then fill or decorate as desired with creams, fruits, etc.

Ingredients for 4 servings
2⅓ cups plus 1 tbsp (10½ oz or 300 g) all-purpose flour; **3/4** cup (5 oz or 140 g) sugar; salt; **1** egg; **1** egg yolk; **1/2** cup plus 2½ tbsps (5½ oz or 150 g) butter, chopped; **1** tsp vanilla extract (or grated citrus zest, if making fruit tarts)

Method
Mound the flour, sugar and a pinch of salt on a work surface. Make a well in the middle and add the egg and egg yolk, butter and vanilla or zest.
Work into an elastic dough, then wrap in plastic wrap and refrigerate before using. Bake at 350°F (180°C or Gas Mark 4) for about 12 minutes.

Creams and Sauces

For delicious and appealing food, it is absolutely crucial to use colorful and tasty sauces to garnish the finished dishes. Here are some recipes for homemade sauces, perfect for any occasion.

the basic rules
Remember to always have all the necessary ingredients set out on the work surface (except for those which have to stay refrigerated or kept warm) to avoid interrupting the preparation and therefore lengthening the resting time of the dough.

Radicchio Sauce

Ingredients for 4 servings

3 tbsps extra-virgin olive oil; **1/2** white onion, minced; **2** heads Treviso radicchio, chopped; **1** tsp red wine vinegar; **1** tsp sugar; salt and pepper

Method

Heat the oil in a saucepan and sauté the onion over heat without browning it. When soft, add the radicchio, and the vinegar.

Sprinkle with sugar and leave to cook for 10 minutes, seasoning with salt and pepper. Transfer to a cutting board and chop finely, then let cool.

Ham Mousse

Ingredients for 4 servings

1 lb (450 g) ham, chopped; **4½** tbsps (2½ oz or 70 g) butter; **2½** tbsps all-purpose flour; **1/2** cup (120 ml) milk; salt and pepper; grated nutmeg; **3/4** cup plus **1** tbsp heavy cream

Method

Puree the ham in a food processor. Melt a tab of butter in a saucepan. Remove from the heat and stir in the flour. Mix then return to the heat. Add the milk and let boil for 3 minutes.

Season with salt and pepper and a sprinkling of nutmeg. Stir in the ham and pass through a sieve. Whip the cream and beat the butter until creamy. Mix the cream and butter into the ham mixture. Pour into a mold and refrigerate for 3-4 hours.

alternatively...
Spread the radicchio sauce on vegetable sandwiches or use it as an accompaniment to a cheese plate.

Guacamole

Ingredients for 4 servings
1 avocado; juice of **1** lemon; **2** spring onions, minced; **1/2** garlic clove, minced; **3** drops of Tabasco; salt and pepper; **1** tomato, deseeded and diced

Method
Halve the avocado, peel off the skin, remove the pit and roughly chop the flesh. Place in a bowl and squeeze over the lemon juice. Add the spring onion, garlic and Tabasco and adjust salt and pepper. Stir in the tomatoes. Serve with corn chips, tortillas or small, crisp toasts.

Salmon Cream

Ingredients for 4 servings
3 oz (80 g) smoked salmon, minced; **1** onion, minced; **7** oz (200 g) robiola cheese; **1/2** tsp paprika; salt

Method
Mix together all the ingredients. Refrigerate for 1 hour. Use to fill tartlets.

Herbed Yogurt

Ingredients for 4 servings
1¾ cups (400 ml) Greek yogurt, sieved; **2** tbsps minced fresh herbs (parsley, dill, oregano, basil); **2** garlic cloves; **2** tbsps honey; **1** tsp salt; pepper

Method
Mix together all the ingredients. Refrigerate overnight. Serve with vegetables.

another idea...
For a more authentic Mexican guacamole add minced cilantro, chile peppers or more garlic to give a more intense and spicy flavor.

basic tools

Finger Foods

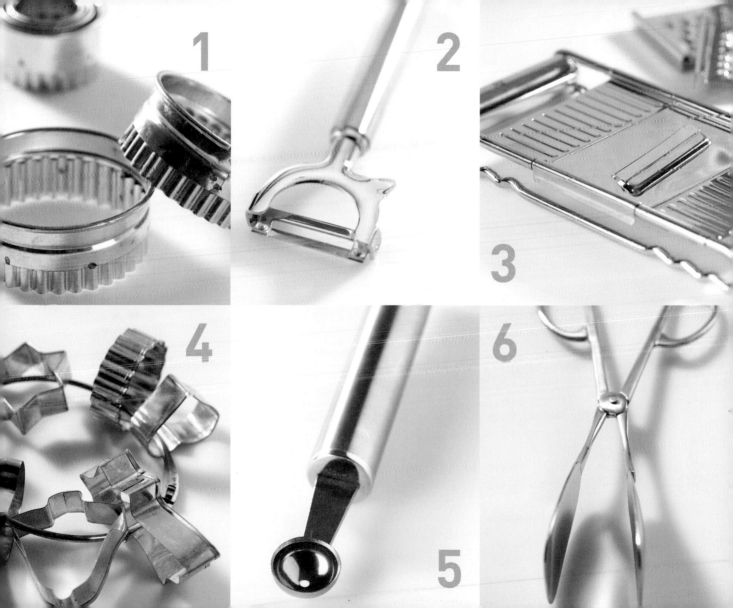

1 Round cookie cutters A fundamental tool for cutting out pastry to line tartlet molds or to make cookies.

2 Vegetable peeler Another very useful kitchen tool, good for peeling carrots, potatoes and zucchini, as well as apples and pears.

3 Grater and slicer Used for making thin carrot ribbons or grating hard cheeses, to make salads tastier and more attractive.

4 Shaped cookie cutters For cutting out unusual shapes. They can be made from tin or stainless steel and are indispensable for making perfect cookies. So as not to ruin the edge, they should be stored in a plastic box after use.

5 Melon baller When appetizers or desserts have to be appealing to the eye as well as the palate, the right tools are essential. Melon ballers can be used to make perfect balls of all kinds of fruit and vegetables.

6 Serving tongs Used for serving pastries like beignets and cannoncini as well as canapés and tartines. For serving guests with a professional touch.

7 Scoring tool Its principal function is to poke holes in pastry before baking, to prevent the pastry puffing up during cooking or forming air bubbles.

8 Individual molds In tin, black cast iron or aluminum, smooth or fluted, for preparing individual little tartlets.

9 Cannoncini molds Usually in aluminum, in different shapes and sizes. Pastry is rolled around the mold and then baked or fried to create tubes which can then be filled.

10 **Flat whisk** This unusual shape is good for whisking small quantities. Perfect for emulsifying vinaigrettes, liquid sauces, creams and also soft omelets.

11 **Rolling cutter** Useful for cutting dough. Can be simple or with several blades with an adjustable distance between them. This allows for dough to be easily cut into identically sized strips.

12 **Parmesan wedge** Strong and solid, in steel, for easily cutting Parmesan or other hard cheeses into chunks. Don't forget that Parmesan makes one of the simplest and also best appetizers around.

13 **Paring knife** For cutting fruits and vegetables into particular shapes, ideal for little tarts filled with vegetables or fruits.

14 **Pastry bag** Used for all kinds of appetizers and desserts in which sauces and creams must be either piped into beignets or used in attractive garnishes.

15 **Special papers** Aluminum and plastic wrap are the best for preserving creams and sweet and savory foods prior to serving. Parchment and waxed paper are indispensable for baking cookies and tartlets without having them stick to the baking sheet.

16 **Aluminum containers** In every shape and size for cooking or reheating dishes in the most practical and quick way.

17 **Pizza wheel** For cleanly cutting even the most crispy pastry.

18 **Small balloon whisk** Small and round, made from steel, perfect for eliminating lumps in liquids in narrow containers.

index

Finger Foods

Savory

Sweet

Fireside
A Division of Simon & Schuster, Inc.
1230 Avenue of the Americas
New York, NY 10020

Published originally under the title *Stuzzichini & Co.*
Copyright © 2005 Food Editore srl
Via Bordoni, 8 - 20124 MILAN
Via Mazzini, 6 - 43100 PARMA
www.foodeditore.it

English Translation by
Traduzioni Culinarie

Photographs by
Alberto Rossi and Davide Di Prato

Recipes by
Simone Rugiati and Licia Cagnoni

First Fireside hardcover edition September 2008

FIRESIDE and colophon are registered trademarks of Simon & Schuster, Inc.

For information about special discounts for bulk purchases, please contact Simon & Schuster Special Sales
at 1-800-456-6798 or business@simonandschuster.com.

Manufactured in the United States of America

10 9 8 7 6 5 4 3 2 1

ISBN-13: 978-1-4165-9345-4
ISBN-10:   1-4165-9345-4